ISLAMIC FUNDAMENTALISM AND MODERNITY

ISLAMIC FUNDAMENTALISM AND MODERNITY

PROFESSOR
WILLIAM MONTGOMERY WATT
Emeritus Professor of Arabic and Islamic Studies
University of Edinburgh

ROUTLEDGE
London and New York

First published in 1988 by Routledge
11 New Fetter Lane, London EC4P 4EE
29 West 35th Street, New York NY 10001

Phototypeset in Linotron Baskerville, 10/12pt
by Input Typesetting Ltd, London
Printed in Great Britain by
T.J. Press (Padstow) Ltd, Padstow, Cornwall

British Library Cataloguing in Publication Data
Watt, W. Montgomery (William Montgomery),
1909–
Islamic fundamentalism and modernity.
1. Islam
I. Title
297

Library of Congress Cataloging in Publication Data
Watt, W. Montgomery (William Montgomery)
Islamic fundamentalism and modernity/William Montgomery Watt.
p. cm.
Bibliography: p.
Includes index.
1. Islam—20th century. I. Title.
BP60.W37 1988
297′.09′04—dc19 88–4386

ISBN 0–415–00623–6

CONTENTS

Chapter One

THE TRADITIONAL SELF-IMAGE OF ISLAM

The central theme of this book is that the thinking of the fundamentalist Islamic intellectuals and of the great masses of ordinary Muslims is still dominated by the standard traditional Islamic world-view and the corresponding self-image of Islam. This is a fact of great importance at the present time when the influence of Islam is increasing throughout the world, since it means that how contemporary problems are seen by many Muslims may be different from how they look to Western observers and statesmen.

A prominent liberal Muslim intellectual, Mohammed Arkoun, has emphasized this point by using the categories of the thinkable, the unthinkable and the unthought (*pensable, impensable, impensé*).[1] In a recent article, after noting that 'the principal philosphical problems developed in the West since the 16th century are [among Muslims] put away into [the category of] the *unthinkable* by the fact of the absence (or elimination) of philosophical reflection after Averroes (Ibn Rushd)', he adds in a footnote:

> Today ideological control confirms this *unthinkable* for everything connected with Islam. It is always impossible to *think* the historicity of the Qur'ān, of the Ḥadīth, of the Sharīʿa, since one would be touching on the foundations of actual powers. That is why 'the resurgence of Islam', which is spoken of by observers who pay attention only to the voices who 'cry out', is taking place on the basis of an immense *unthought* accumulated over centuries. And this *unthought* has become a very illuminating dimension of the conflicts and convulsions which agitate these societies. It is urgent to open analytical thinking (*l'analyse*) to these data, which in no way go back only to speculative

> philosophy, since it could be that Muslims themselves are stumbling against the *unthinkable* and the *unthought* as over obstacles bequeathed by their own history, and that in this there is one of the deep but secret reasons for so many current problems.[2]

By 'thinking the historicity of the Qur'ān . . .' the author seems to mean seeing its assertions as historical facts to which the methods of historical criticism may properly be applied. This, of course, is only one small area of the *unthinkable* and *unthought*, since, as will be seen in what follows, the standard world-view covers virtually the whole of life.

This standard or traditional world-view may be said to have been established in its main lines by about the year AD 950 and certainly by 1200. Since then it has remained unchanged. Earlier deviant sectarian views have mostly been squeezed out, and there has been little opportunity for novel sectarian views to develop. A movement like Wahhābism, which appeared in central Arabia in the eighteenth century and is now the official teaching of the Sa'udi kingdom, though novel in a sense, is essentially a reinforcement of some aspects of the standard world-view in a conservative direction.

Because of popular journalistic usage it has been thought convenient to retain the term 'fundamentalist' in the title of this book although it is inexact. It is primarily an Anglo-Saxon Protestant term, especially applied to those who hold that the Bible must be accepted and interpreted literally. The nearest French equivalent is *intégrisme*, which refers to a similar but by no means identical tendency within Roman Catholicism. In Islam Sunnite fundamentalists accept the Qur'ān literally, though in some cases with qualifications,[3] but they have also other distinctive features. The Shī'ites of Iran, who in a very general sense are fundamentalists, are not committed to a literal interpretation of the Qur'ān.

For the purposes of this book the important distinction is between those Muslims who fully accept the traditional world-view and want to maintain it intact and those who see that it needs to be corrected in some respects. The former group are the fundamentalists, but will here be spoken of rather as conservatives and traditionalists, while the latter group will be referred to as liberals.

Among both groups, but especially among the former, many different political movements and attitudes are to be found. The ulema or religious scholars, who are the primary bearers and transmitters of the traditional world-view, are mostly reactionary in the sense that they tend to oppose reforms. Among those here called conservatives and traditionalists, however, there is also a bewildering variety of reformist elements, and these are sometimes very critical of the ulema. The reforms they are interested in are nearly all social and political, and leave the traditional world-view unchanged. The liberals are interested not only in changing the world-view, but also in other reforms.

The remainder of this chapter is devoted to a presentation in outline of the traditional world-view concentrating on those aspects of it which affect the policy and praxis of Islamic states and of individual Muslims.

1 THE UNCHANGING STATIC WORLD

For Muslims unchangingness is both an ideal for human individuals and societies, and also a perception of the actual nature of humanity and its environment. Unchangingness is an all-pervading assumption which colours most aspects of the standard world-view, and this justifies giving it a prominent place in the presentation. Moreover, it is something which a Westerner finds it difficult to appreciate without a deliberate effort of thought. The idea of development is part of our general intellectual outlook. Anyone over the age of thirty has seen great changes in their lifetime, and assumes that these changes are for the better. In the case of the machines and gadgets which we are using in ever-increasing numbers we tend to expect a new and *improved* version every few years. Even if some of us are more critical of the idea of progress than our Victorian ancestors were, we still suppose that human society has advanced not just since primitive times but even from the eighteenth and nineteenth centuries. It is thus very difficult for the Westerner to appreciate the outlook of those in whose thinking there is no place for development, progress or social advance and improvement.

It was in my studies of the Islamic sects that I first became aware of the complete absence of the idea of development. In Islam there are no official creeds such as are found in Christianity, since there are no bodies authorized to make a particular creed the official creed of all Muslims; but in the formulation of credal doctrines there has come to be a wide area of informal consensus. Many scholars have formulated creeds, and when the modern Western observer looks at these he sees a process of development, because new or more precise clauses were added to make clear the falsity of views put forward by sectarian deviants. Traditional Muslim scholars of these matters, however, do not admit this development, but claim that true doctrine in its entirety was present from the time of Muḥammad himself. The various sects, too, are seen simply as people who accepted false views, and the falsity is demonstrated. There is no realization that some of the sectarians made important contributions to Muslim thinking on religious matters. The early sect of Khārijites, for example, insisted on certain practical decisions being based on Qur'ānic principles, although at the time many Muslim leaders tended rather to follow pre-Islamic Arab custom: and this Khārijite doctrine, after the Sunna of the Prophet had been added to the Qur'ān, became standard Sunnite teaching. Later Muslim writers on the sects, however, emphasize those views of the sectarians which came to be regarded as false, and seem incapable of thinking that the sects could have made any positive contribution.

There are many other spheres beside theology, however, in which Muslim thinkers show no conception of development. They hold that in the centuries since Muḥammad human beings have not changed in essentials. There may indeed have been variations of several kinds but these have been as much down as up, and there cannot be said to have been any advances or progress in human character. This unchangingness of human nature, as they see it, justifies Muslim scholars in asserting the finality of the rules and laws for human conduct which are expressed in the Qur'ān and the Sunna of the Prophet. Since human nature does not change, there can in essentials be no new problems, and therefore no need for any fundamental revision of the Sharīʿa. The idea of social reform is thus virtually unthinkable for traditionally minded Muslims.

It is worth looking further at this concept of the unchangingness of human nature. Despite their belief in development modern Western observers will, if they are honest, admit that there is much in the world today to suggest that human beings are in general no better than they were fourteen hundred years ago. We need only think of the atrocities against Jews and others committed in Hitler's Reich, of the oppression of the masses in Latin America by the wealthy and powerful, of the invention and use of the nuclear bomb, or of the exploitation of the Third World by vast multinational Western corporations. There is still much wickedness in human nature at its core. Once this has been admitted, however, there are still other points to be considered. Thus it would seem that the number of persons comprised in a body politic affects the quality of their social life. We describe life in small political units (such as the nomadic tribes of Arabs in Muḥammad's time) as primitive, and we contrast this with civilized life, where there are much larger units (such as the Roman empire or the ʿAbbāsid caliphate) and where a measure of peace, security and social justice is maintained. The original elaboration of the Sharīʿa during the first three centuries or so of Islam did in fact adapt to a civilized empire what had been at first the practice of a relatively primitive community.

A more fundamental question, however, is whether the scientific and technological advances of the West, especially during the last two centuries, have altered the nature of human society; and it would seem that the answer is in the affirmative, even if the human individual is capable of being as wicked as ever. Advances in the speed of travel have made it possible for those in authority to exercise control over much larger numbers of their human brothers and sisters. The invention of radio and television makes it possible for a few people to control the thinking of vast populations, and makes it difficult to insulate any part of the world from what is happening elsewhere. Consequently, even if it is admitted that human nature has not changed in essentials, there have been changes in human society which require changes in law. Thus the traditional assumption by Muslims of the unchangingness of human nature blinds them to the new problems created for human society by technological advances.

Another particular area in which Muslims assume absence of change is philosophical speculation. Traditionalist Muslims today like to claim that 'Islam is a religion based on reason';[4] but if asked to elaborate this point, they can only produce the sort of philosophical reasoning that was in vogue in the twelfth century. As Mohammed Arkoun indicated, they know of no philosophy since Averroes, and are completely unaware of the new challenges to religious belief produced by men like Hume and Feuerbach, not to mention our twentieth-century philosophers. Whether philosophy has advanced is perhaps debatable, but it is certainly not static.

The acceptance of unchangingness as both a fact and an ideal probably goes back to the Arab experience of nomadic life, as a result of which it was held that safety consisted in following the 'beaten track' (*sunna*) of the ancestors. The nomads of Arabia were undoubtedly aware of change. Tribes were successful and flourished, increased in numbers, then experienced misfortunes, declined and sometimes disappeared altogether; but such variations did not mean that life was changing in essentials. It was therefore better to do as 'the fathers' had always done, since that had in many cases led to satisfactory results. The climate of Arabia was erratic, and the eventualities of desert life unpredictable, so that the nomad could not avoid disaster by making careful plans, but rather schooled himself to accept whatever fate determined for him. Such an outlook made following 'the beaten track' the soundest option. Anything novel was liable to be suspect. The Qur'ān (46.9) is careful to emphasize that Muḥammad's call to be a prophet was not a novelty (*bidʿ*), but that he came after a long line of prophets and messengers. In later Islamic theology the usual word for heresy was 'innovation' (*bidʿa*). Another point is that in desert travel one is less likely to lose one's way if one follows the 'beaten track' (if there is one), and this may also have contributed to the religious usages.[5]

Christian writers on Islam have sometimes taken the view that Muslims are more otherworldly in their outlook than Christians, and think more of the world to come than of attaining an ideal condition of society in this world. Whether this is so or not is unclear, though the readiness of young Iranians to face martyrdom in the war with Iraq is impressive evidence. In so far as there is truth in the view that Muslims are more otherworldly, it links up with the concept of the unchangeableness of human nature and the absence of any belief that humanity is capable of developing towards an intrinsically better form of society.

2 THE FINALITY OF ISLAM

Islam claims that it is the final religion, and that it contains in the Qur'ān and the Sunna all the essential religious and moral truth required by the whole human race from now until the end of time. It holds that all theological truth was present from the first, though it admits that the Sharīʿa was gradually elaborated over the first three centuries of Islam by suitably qualified religious scholars, those now known as ulema (*ʿulamā'*). When the Islamic state expanded into provinces of the Byzantine and Persian empires, new problems had to be faced which had not been encountered during Muḥammad's lifetime. The Qur'ān and the Sunna, however, contained the principles on which such problems could be solved. For example, the ulema could argue that the ground (*'illa*) of the Qur'ānic prohibition of wine (*khamr*) was that it led to intoxication; and it then followed that, when some hitherto unknown beverage, like gin or whisky, became available and proved to be intoxicating, it was likewise prohibited. It is on this basis that Islam claims to have all moral and and religious truth necessary for all humanity. The claim is all the more convincing to traditional Muslims in that they do not expect human society to develop in any essential way.

The claim to finality is also supported by a Qur'ānic verse (33.40) in which Muḥammad is described as 'the seal of the prophets' (*khāṭam an-nabiyyīn*). To the first hearers this probably meant that Muḥammad was the seal which confirmed the truth of previous prophets, but it is now universally interpreted by Muslims to mean that Muḥammad is the last of the prophets, after whom there will be no other. This interpretation is the basis of the recent Pakistani declaration that members of the Ahmadiyya community are not Muslims, since at least some of them hold that their founder, Mirza Ghulam Ahmad, was a prophet.[6]

The claim that Islam is the final religion is supported by assertions about Judaism and Christianity, the two religions with which the early Muslim community was most in contact. The Qur'ān has verses (e.g. 5.44–8) which acknowledge Moses and Jesus as the prophets who founded Judaism and Christianity respectively. It assumes that the revelations which they received from God were in essentials identical with the teaching of the Qur'ān and were confirmed by that. After the Hijra, however, when Muslims came to have more contacts with the Jews of Medina, they realized that there were differences both in doctrinal matters and in points of law. In the Qur'ān various accusations are made, especially against the Jews, such as that 'they altered the words from their sets' (4.46). In this verse the word translated 'sets' (*mawāḍi'*) can mean either 'places' or 'meanings', but, whatever the original interpretation, the point underlying this and similar accusations is the belief that the Jews knowingly concealed the fact that there were passages in their scripture which clearly foretold the coming of a prophet such as Muḥammad. Other Qur'ānic verses seem to show that the Jews also made fun of Muḥammad by verbal tricks.

While these seem to be the most serious charges against the Jews actually made in the Qur'ān, Muslim scholars in the first century of Islam used the Qur'ānic verses to elaborate a theory of the complete 'corruption' (or 'alteration') of the Jewish and Christian scriptures; they relied particularly on verses with the word 'alter' (*yuḥarrifūna*), of which the word usually translated 'corruption' (*taḥrīf*) is the verbal noun. It was not clear whether this was corruption of the text or only of the meaning; but this indefiniteness did not reduce the efficacy of the theory in preventing Jews and Christians arguing with Muslims on the basis of the Bible. Since the Bible was regarded as corrupt, it could not be used in serious argument. Although it was mainly the Jews who had been criticized in the Qur'ān in this way, the New Testament was also held to be corrupted.

This theory or doctrine of the corruption of the scriptures still dominates the thinking of traditionally-minded Muslims. They are ready to admit that all religious communities based on revelation have received the one and same true religion, but they make this assertion on the basis of what they have learnt from the Qur'ān, and without any evidence from a study of the actual views of the adherents of these religions. Then they go on to claim that, since the other traditions have been corrupted, it is irrational to adhere to them after the coming of the Qur'ān. The same people usually admit that the other religions had Sharī'āt or systems of law different from that of Islam, and then maintain either that these have been abrogated by the Islamic Sharī'a, or that they are dependent on corrupt scriptures.

3 THE SELF-SUFFICIENCY OF ISLAM

A story symbolizing the self-sufficiency of Islam according to Muslim belief was given publicity by Edward Gibbon in his *Decline and Fall of the Roman Empire* (ch.51). When an Arab army conquered and occupied Alexandria in 641, they found the famous library with its vast collection of books. The Arab general sent a message to the caliph 'Umar in Medina informing him of his success and asking what was to be done with the library. He received the reply, 'If the books are in accordance with the Qur'ān, they are unnecessary and may be destroyed; if they contradict the Qur'ān, they are dangerous and should certainly be destroyed.' The general acted accordingly, and the bath-houses of Alexandria are reported to have been heated for months by the precious volumes. Gibbon himself was inclined to doubt the truth of the story, and modern historians regard it as definitely apocryphal, since there are grounds for thinking that the library had been moved away from Alexandria many years previously. The attitude described by the story, however, is by no means apocryphal and is still alive at the present day.

The story doubtless gained currency among Muslims after many Christians had been incorporated into the Islamic empire as 'protected minorities' (*dhimmīs*) and had criticized the Qur'ān as being a pale reflection of Jewish and Christian ideas. Muslims in the nineteenth century had somewhat similar attitudes when Western scholars tried to show that the Qur'ān was dependent on Jewish and Christian sources. For Muslims the Qur'ān was the speech of God transmitted to Muḥammad by the angel Gabriel, and God could not be subject to any cultural or literary influences. This is still the belief of the traditionalists.

The idea of the self-sufficiency of Islam seems to have come from the first or second generation of Muslims after Muḥammad and not from the Qur'ān itself. It is obvious to the modern Western scholar that the intellectual outlook of seventh-century Mecca was permeated with Jewish and Christian ideas. Muḥammad himself, too, was aware that many of the matters spoken of in the Qur'ān were familiar to Jews and Christians, but he did not see any problem in this. While he was still in Mecca opponents accused him of receiving the content of the Qur'ān from other people, presumably persons with some knowledge of the Bible (25.4f). When the accusation is refuted, however, the existence of such a person seems to be admitted, but the point is made that he could not have produced the Qur'ānic verses since he is a foreigner (16.103).[7] In other words, because of the way in which the revelations came to him – from God without any human agency – it was obvious to Muḥammad that no borrowing had taken place, even though there were parallels with Jewish and Christian teaching.

After the incorporation of Christians into the Islamic empire as protected minorities some of these seem to have been saying that the Qur'ān often copied Biblical stories, and sometimes did so inaccurately, as when it denied the death of Jesus on the cross (4.157–9). Against the charge that Muḥammad had copied from previous scriptures Muslims developed the doctrine of Muḥammad's illiteracy, which implied his complete inability to read the scriptures. The doctrine was based on the application to Muḥammad in the Qur'ān of the adjective *ummī*, which was alleged to mean 'illiterate'. The word occurs a number of times in the Qur'ān in both singular and plural, and appears to have been taken from the Jews and to mean 'non-Jewish' or 'Gentile' or 'unscriptured'. Modern Western scholars, though regarding the argument for Muḥammad's illiteracy as somewhat dubious, would certainly admit that he had never read the Bible and had never even received any precise idea of its contents from any oral source. They would thus agree that in the Qur'ān there is no conscious borrowing from other scriptures; but they would attribute the parallels between the Qur'ān and the Bible as due to the presence in the intellectual environment of Muḥammad and the first Muslims of elements from Jewish and Christian tradition.

The insistence on the self-sufficiency of Islam over against Judaism and Christianity is probably bound up with pre-Islamic nomadic attitudes. In nomadic life there were strong tribes and weak tribes. A strong tribe prided itself on being able to maintain its existence against all hostile tribes. Weak tribes were unable to do this, and therefore had to rely on support and 'protection' from a strong tribe. When groups of Jews and Christians come into the Islamic state as protected minorities, they were roughly in the position of weak tribes protected by the strong tribe of the Muslim community. It would thus have been somewhat ignominious for the strong tribe of Muslims to admit dependence in any sense on the weak tribes of Jews and Christians.

This point helps to explain another feature of the elaboration of the idea of Islamic self-sufficiency, namely, unwillingness to admit the existence of borrowing where it had in fact taken place. In the Sīra or biography of Muḥammad by Ibn-Isḥāq (d.768), which is our main primary source for his life, Muḥammad is given a genealogy going back to Adam, but it is not mentioned that the earlier part of this is derived from the Bible. Similarly Biblical material is found without acknowledgment in the sayings attributed to Muḥammad (Ḥadīth). He is said, for example, to have recommended the use of a prayer which, though omitting the word 'father', contains most of the clauses of the Christian Lord's Prayer.[8] Most interesting is the report that Muḥammad once said that 'God created Adam in his image' (*ṣūra*), echoing Genesis 1.27. Some

Muslim scholars were aware that this came from the Bible, and were prepared to accept it in the sense which it obviously has there, namely, that God created Adam in his (God's) image; but this interpretation was eventually rejected by the consensus of Muslim scholars, and various ways were found of interpreting the words in some other sense, such as 'in Adam's own proper image'. Most ingenious was the alleged report that Muḥammad once passed a man beating his slave and told him to desist because 'God made Adam in his (the slave's) image'.[9] The rejection of the Biblical interpretation may have been due in part to the fact that it was Biblical, but it may also have owed something to Islamic insistence on the transcendence of God, and to the suggestion in the word *ṣūra* of a compositeness which could in no way be ascribed to God.

Once it had been generally accepted that the scriptures had been corrupted, few Muslim scholars showed any interest in studying the Bible. There was no attempt to compare the Qur'ānic version of the stories of Noah, Joseph and the like with the Biblical account; and indeed one can see that to have attempted this might have led to dangerous questionings. A few Muslim scholars looked at the Bible in order to find verses foretelling the prophethood of Muḥammad and, as they alleged, found a large number. Others at various periods studied the New Testament to get arguments against Christian claims. This was virtually all, however. In the first century some material derived from two Jewish scholars who had become Muslims was used in the interpretation of the Qur'ān, but as time went on material from Jewish sources came to be regarded with suspicion. In the first third of the present century there were Egyptian scholars who argued that material from the above-mentioned Muslims of Jewish origin should not be accepted, not even when it was included in the collections of 'sound' Ḥadīth.[10] Such is the extent of the continuing belief in the purity of Islam and the danger of incorporating non-Islamic elements. This suspicion of the non-Islamic has come to be attached even more firmly to Christian philosophical and religious teaching, that is, to most of modern Western thought. This point will be illustrated more fully later in the book.

The suspicion of everything non-Islamic was for a time extended to the vocabulary of the Qur'ān, and attempts were made to prove that words like *dīnār* (a coin) and Jahannam (Hell), which were obviously derived from the Latin *denarius* and the Hebrew Gehenna, originally came from Arabic roots. In the end the more learned Qur'ānic scholars conceded that such words were of foreign origin, but maintained that they had been genuinely accepted into Arabic.

There were two exceptions in the early centuries to this rejection of borrowing from alien cultures, namely, Greek intellectual culture and Iranian culture. When the Arabs conquered Iraq they found colleges which gave instruction in Greek science and philosophy, though the medium of instruction was now Syriac. The Arabs were particularly interested in Greek medicine and astronomy, the latter being useful in their far-flung empire in determining the direction to be faced in prayer (towards Mecca). There were Christian physicians at the ʿAbbāsid court, and, through contact with these and with former students of the colleges who had become Muslims, several Muslim religious scholars became interested in Greek thought, especially philosophy, and saw that it provided weapons they could use against theological adversaries both within the fold of Islam and beyond. Round about the year 800 a number of Greek ideas were brought into relation with Islamic theological doctrine, and this led to the development of Kalām or philosophical theology. This may be called the first wave of Hellenism. Mainstream religious scholars, however, engaged in no further study of Greek thought for nearly three hundred years, when an outstanding theologian al-Ghazālī (d.1111) studied carefully the works in the Greek tradition by that time available in Arabic, notably the writings of the philosopher Ibn-Sīnā, known in the West as Avicenna (d.1037).

In the interval of three hundred years a few Muslims, while claiming to be good Muslims, had adopted an intellectual position which was primarily that of Greek thought, and indeed a form of Neoplatonism. These thinkers are conveniently referred to as the Falāsifa. Al-Ghazālī, after his remarkable achievement of assimilating the thought of the Falāsifa by his private reading of their works, wrote a refutation of their views which contributed to a decline of philosophy in most Islamic regions. In the course of his studies, however, he became greatly impressed by some features of Greek thought. He was particularly impressed by Aristotelian logic and wrote one or two short books on logic which made the subject comprehensible to members of the religious institution. He also introduced further Greek concepts and arguments into Kalām. As a result of his work one finds in the following centuries theological treatises which devote more space to the philosophical preliminaries than to theology proper. Thus in the end Greek philosophy, despite the original enthusiasm of some Muslims for it, only survived where it had assumed an Islamic dress. Other Greek sciences were cultivated for a time by individuals, and useful contributions were made, especially in medicine and pharmacological botany, but in the end these sciences faded away, probably through lack of support from the Islamic community in general.

Something of Iranian culture was accepted into Islam, doubtless because the majority of Iranians became Muslims at an early period. One of the signs of this acceptance is that traditional Iranian history found a place in world histories by Muslim authors, in contrast to their almost complete neglect of Roman history. The Iranian heritage of political wisdom, based on centuries of experience, was also brought into Islam in the form of a genre of literary works commonly known as 'mirrors for princes'.

The belief in the self-sufficiency of Islam, together with the suspicion of all that is not Islamic and the reluctance to borrow from alien cultures, continues at the present time. At the First World Conference on Muslim Education held in Mecca in spring 1977 the main body of participants showed concern over the effects on Muslims of the Western-type education which many receive, and called for new Islamic forms of the natural and social sciences and the humanities, which would be based on concepts drawn from Islam. More will be said about this later. It may be noted here, however, that this attitude is bound up with a particular conception of knowledge. Muḥammad is reported to have said, 'Seek knowledge, even from China,' but, as has just been seen, Muslims were unwilling to seek knowledge even from the alien cultures within their empire. This is probably to be explained by the fact that, when Muslims think of knowledge, they think primarily of what may be called 'knowledge for living', whereas when a Westerner thinks of knowledge it is mainly of 'knowledge for power', that is, such knowledge as enables one to control natural and material objects and human individuals and societies. It is in respect of knowledge for living, consisting of religious and moral values, that Islam claims finality and self-sufficiency.

It should perhaps be noted here that Sir Hamilton Gibb has characterized the medieval Islamic conception of knowledge in a somewhat different way. He writes:

> the old Islamic view of knowledge was not a reaching-out to the unknown but a mechanical process of amassing the 'known'. The known was not conceived of as changing and expanding but as 'given' and eternal. Not everybody, of course, could possess all knowledge, but there was at least a fixed sum of knowledge, most of which was in the possession of some persons or other.[11]

This has been followed to some extent by Fazlur Rahman; speaking of medieval Islamic scholarship he says that it 'is not regarded as an active pursuit, a creative "reaching-out" of the mind to the unknown – as is the case today – but rather as the passive acquisition of already established knowledge.'[12] This way of describing knowledge links up with the unchangingness of human life, and is complementary to the distinction just drawn between knowledge for living and knowledge for power.

The corollary of this traditional conception of knowledge is that Muslims show surprisingly little interest in other forms of knowledge, even those which would be useful to them for practical purposes. Many examples of this will be found in Bernard Lewis's book *The Muslim Discovery of Europe*.[13] Even when the Ottoman empire ruled much of south-eastern Europe and was involved in conflicts with the western European states, its ruling group did not take the trouble to learn some of the elementary facts of European geography. As late as 1770 they did not know that there was open seaway from the Baltic to the Mediterranean. When a Russian fleet appeared in the Mediterranean, the Ottomans thought it must have come through some sort of channel from the Baltic to Venice, and protested to the Venetians because they had allowed the Russians to pass through this channel.

4 ISLAM IN HISTORY

Prior to the coming of Islam the nomadic Arabs had only a very limited historical awareness, and even the urban Arabs were probably not much better informed. They were not greatly interested in anything beyond their own immediate circles. They were aware of how in desert life there could be a rise and decline of tribes. They saw tribes becoming weaker and fading away, while others grew in numbers and importance; and then the latter might also fade away and be replaced by yet others. Slight memories had been preserved, as we learn from the Qur'ān, of the no longer extant tribes of ʿĀd and Thamūd. The historical material known to the pre-Islamic Arabs was mostly in the form of stories about 'the days of the Arabs' (*ayyām al-Arab*), which were primarily the days on which there had been important battles. A rough chronological framework for this material was provided by genealogy, so that the Arabs thought in terms of generations rather than of years and decades. Centuries were beyond their ken. They had no long perspectives, since most tribes had existed for only a few generations. There was no conception of a continuing historical process such as is described in the Bible. This lack of historical awareness may have contributed to the absence of a concept of development.

A little was known in Mecca about Biblical history, and this was made use of in the Qur'ān and perhaps added to. The various Biblical personages and events mentioned there were not presented in historical order; the stories came separately and in haphazard fashion, so that there was no idea of the linear history of the Israelites. This may explain, for example, why in the Qur'ān (19.28) there is apparent confusion between Miriam, the sister of Aaron, and Mary, the mother of Jesus, both of whom are Maryam in Arabic.

Into this formless world Muḥammad was sent by God as a prophet, 'out of the blue', as it were; or, if there was a reason for his being sent when he was sent, it was that the Arabs had never had a prophet – at least not since the time of Abraham and Ishmael who had founded a community at Mecca which had since disappeared. In later passages of the Qur'ān it was claimed that Muḥammad was a prophet for all humanity. Such a view was strengthened by the remarkable successes of the Arab armies in the century after Muḥammad's death. Westwards they had conquered all North Africa, had occupied much of Spain and raided as far as the centre of France. Eastwards they had overrun the Persian empire and penetrated into Central Asia and the Punjab. This expansion of Muḥammad's city-state into an empire was taken to show that the Muslims were continuing to be supported by God, as they had been at the battle of Badr in 624; and it came to be expected that the Islamic empire would expand to include the whole human race.

This expectation or assumption came to be expressed by contrasting 'the sphere of Islam' (*dār al-islām*) with 'the sphere of war' (*dār al-ḥarb*). The sphere of Islam embraces those regions under Islamic rulers in which the provisions of the Islamic Sharīʿa are observed and Muslims can practise their religion, even if there are also non-Muslims with the status of protected minorities, following their own laws in personal matters. The sphere of war consists of the regions and peoples not under Muslim rulers. After the first century of Islam the expansion of the empire was not so steady and continuous, but there were sufficient advances from time to time to offset the occasional withdrawals and maintain belief in the ultimate triumph of the sphere of Islam. After the Ottoman empire had conquered much of south-eastern Europe by the sixteenth century it saw Europe as its 'sphere of war' and itself as extending 'the sphere of Islam'; and this perception seems to have continued, despite loss of territory, at least until nearly the end of the eighteenth century. At the present time something of the belief in the ultimate triumph of Islam seems to be inspiring much of the foreign policy of Ayatollah Khomeini.

In this conception of Islamic history the point that is important for non-Muslim states is not the belief in the ultimate domination of Islam, but the fact that in the present there are difficulties in Islamic states having permanent treaties with non-Muslims. The medieval jurists held that a treaty with a state or ruler in the sphere of war should not be for longer than ten years. Modern Muslim statesmen have, of course, entered into binding agreements with non-Muslims – in the United Nations, for example – but this practice has never been sanctioned by the traditional exponents of the Sharīʿa. Thus the division of the world into the sphere of Islam and the sphere of war is by no means a thing of the past. In so far as traditionalist Islam grows in strength it could come into the forefront of world politics.

A side-effect of the Western education received by many Muslims during the last century or so, and in particular of their study of European history, has been their realization that the colonialism from which Muslim countries have suffered in recent times was in part parallel to the occupation of Palestine and some surrounding regions by the Crusaders in the eleventh and twelfth centuries. The significance of the Crusades for Muslims and for Christians was in fact very different. The actual Crusaders were supported by a great tide of religious fervour in Western Europe, and religious aims were uppermost in the minds of most of them. For the Muslims in general, however, the Crusades were of little concern, a mere series of local incidents. For those involved they could, of course, be a matter of life and death, but even these Muslims probably saw them as little more than a continuation of the Byzantine raids with which they had long been familiar, though they soon came to distinguish Franks from Byzantines. The caliph in Baghdad was informed of the Frankish invasion but showed no interest; and the main power in the Islamic world at that time, the Seljuq dynasty, had its chief centres hundreds of miles to the east of Baghdad and possibly did not even know of the Crusades. Some Muslims today, however, see various forms of Western aggression against the Islamic world as a recrudescence of the crusading movement. Colonel Qadhafi of Libya goes so far as to speak of Napoleon's invasion of Egypt in 1798 as the Ninth Crusade and the establishment of the state of Israel with American support as the Tenth Crusade. This last is somewhat inappropriate, since the aim of most of the original Crusaders was to bring the Christian holy places under Christian control.

5 THE IDEALIZATION OF MUHAMMAD AND EARLY ISLAM

Associated with this perception of the place of Islam in world history was an idealizing and romanticizing of Muḥammad and the early Muslims. Muḥammad was held to be perfect in every way, and never to have been a pagan, despite the fact that the Qur'ān (93.7) speaks of him as 'erring' (*ḍāll*), and other sources report that he had sacrificed to the local deities. This idealization of Muḥammad leads modern Muslims to reject the story of the 'satanic verses' although it is accepted by the eminent historian and exegete aṭ-Ṭabarī and has some support from a verse in the Qur'ān (22.52). The story is that on one occasion, while Muḥammad was hoping that he might receive a revelation which would bring over to his side the leaders of Quraysh hostile to him, Satan inserted verses into the revelation permitting intercession to three local goddesses. Muḥammad thought these verses were part of the genuine revelation, proclaimed them publicly, and was joined by the Meccan leaders in an act of Islamic worship. Later he realized that he had been mistaken about these verses and proclaimed a revised form, not allowing intercession, and thus caused the Meccans to turn away from him. It seems impossible that any Muslim could have invented this story, or that aṭ-Ṭabarī would have accepted it from a non-Muslim. Yet most traditionalist Muslims today reject it.

This process of idealization was not restricted to Muḥammad himself and his Companions, but extended to the whole period of the first four 'rightly guided' caliphs, the Rāshidūn, and further. Thus it is supposed that the men in the early Muslim armies were motivated chiefly by zeal for Islam and for its spread, though this is not borne out by an objective look at the historical sources. The expeditions did not at first lead to conversions on any great scale (except in Iran), since the status of 'protected minorities' was given to most of the inhabitants of the occupied territories. The primary aim of most of the expeditions – like that into France in 732 which was defeated at Tours – was the acquiring of booty, and this is doubtless what was uppermost in the minds of the troops. Muslims today sometimes claim that the early Islamic conquests were not a 'colonial phenomenon' but 'conquests in the field of creed and the construction of the human personality', though the writer from whom these phrases are quoted somewhat contradictorily asserts that Islam did not spread by the sword.[14]

Another aspect of the idealization of the early Muslims is the view that their religious devotion was such that they remembered the verses of the Qur'ān perfectly and that, when they copied it as scribes, they never made mistakes. Ordinary Muslims today will argue that there are no textual variants for the Qur'ān as there are for the Bible. The scholars, however, are well aware that there are seven (or some other number) sets of readings, all of which are accepted as canonical, in accordance with a Ḥadīth to the effect that God revealed the Qur'ān according to seven *ḥurūf* (literally 'letters'). They thus maintain that what the Western scholar sees as textual variants are not variants but alternative forms of genuine revelation. Modern Western scholars have in addition drawn attention to works by medieval Muslim scholars which contained lists of non-canonical textual variants which were in circulation prior to the standardizing of the text of the Qur'ān in the caliphate of ʿUthmān about 650.

There were also idealized accounts of the lives of some of the early Muslims. In particular there was a group known as Ahl aṣ-Ṣuffa, who were models of poverty and piety and had no home other than the *ṣuffa* or covered portico of the mosque at Medina (which adjoined Muḥammad's house). There are said to have been as many as 400 of these men, according to later accounts. To judge from the early sources, however, the reality was quite different. There is no evidence of people living permanently in the *ṣuffa*. Men from outside Medina, not necessarily poor, but with no confederate in the city to house them, may have slept there while on a brief visit; and Muḥammad may occasionally have invited poor men to share his meal there; but that seems to have been about all. The account of the Ahl aṣ-Ṣuffa was no doubt circulated and expanded by later Muslims who disapproved of the material luxury of some of their contemporaries.[15]

There is even a sense in which the whole of Islamic history may be said to have been idealized by the traditionalists, or at least moulded according to 'the demands of religious emotion and theological dogma' as Sir Hamilton Gibb has phrased it.[16] Up to the tenth century AD the historians had employed critical methods, but after that point history became subordinated to the interests of the ulema, who regarded it as 'an instrument of moral instruction and of dogmatic controversy'. The version of history accepted by the ulema then became part of the standard Islamic world-view from which any deviation was regarded as heresy.

The modern Western observer cannot fail to be aware of great dangers inherent in the idealization of early Islam. There is a sense in which it is similar to the Christian slogan of 'Back to the Bible' which has been used as a rallying-cry for reform; but there is an important difference. The forms of life depicted in the Bible cover many centuries, and Christian reformers were selective in what they imitated. It was chiefly some aspects of the New Testament that were followed, and there was no question of copying the crudities of the Old Testament. In Islam, however, the idea of going back to the Qur'ān and the example of Muḥammad means the idealization of a period of little more than twenty years in a region of the world where life was still somewhat primitive and barbaric. Nearly all Westerners, whether God-fearing or not, are horrified that Muslims of today can contemplate the amputation of a hand as a punishment for theft or stoning as a punishment for adultery, even if only in a few precisely defined cases.

The amputation of the thief's hand is certainly prescribed in the Qur'ān (5.58), and was presumably sometimes carried out. In a modern society this would make a man or woman incapable of earning a living honestly and instead become a burden on the community; and one can only think that in Muḥammad's time the person thus punished would have had some sort of family support, and that it may have been felt appropriate that the whole family should suffer for the fault of one member.

Stoning for adultery is not a punishment prescribed in the Qur'ān according to the standard text. One verse (4.15) speaks of a guilty woman not being allowed to leave the house; and a later verse (24.2) says that a guilty man and woman are both to be flogged. There are reports, however, that the caliph ʿUmar maintained that they had once recited a 'verse of stoning', prescribing this punishment, as part of the Qur'ān; and the text is extant.[17] There are also reports that Muḥammad had sometimes carried out the punishment. From the standpoint of modern historical criticism both the story about ʿUmar and the reports about Muḥammad are almost certainly to be rejected. There are several grounds for this, but the decisive argument is that in Mecca and even more in Medina in pre-Islamic times many strange forms of 'marital' relationship were found, such as polyandry (one woman having several 'husbands'), and these forms were regarded as socially acceptable.[18] One of the aims of the Qur'ānic rules was to ensure that a woman had sexual relations with only one man at a time; but it seems to have been realised that this ideal could not be achieved all at once, since it was contrary to many hitherto normal practices. The Qur'ān thus seems to distinguish between women who accept and observe the restriction to one man (whom it calls *muḥṣināt* or *muḥṣanāt*) and those who do not observe the restriction. All this makes it difficult to know what the *zinā'* (translated 'adultery') could have been for which stoning was prescribed. The verse (24.3) following that prescribing flogging speaks of the 'adulterer' being allowed to marry only an 'adultress' or an idolatress; and this might be taken to imply that there was a class of practitioners of *zinā'* (meaning something traditionally allowed) who were now partly (?) excluded from the community of Muslims though continuing to live among them.

The conclusion to which this points is that there was no stoning for adultery in Islam until a least a generation after Muḥammad, by which time the earlier polyandric practices had faded out and been forgotten. The acceptance of stoning may have come about because of Jewish criticisms that the Qur'ān was not so strict about adultery as the Bible, where death is the punishment.[19] Though stoning is not specifically mentioned in these passages, it is known from the New Testament[20] and other sources that the punishment was often carried out by stoning. In a society where the *lex talionis* is still in operation, stoning is a way of preventing any single person from incurring blood-guilt for the death. The introduction into the Sharīʿa of stoning as a punishment for adultery must have been the work of Muslim religious scholars in the latter half of the first Islamic century, but it is difficult to know the precise social circumstances with which they were concerned. What can be said here is that in accepting stoning as a possible punishment for adultery Muslims of today are idealizing not the earliest Islam as it really was, but as it was alleged to have been by later scholars.

It also seems incredible that in the later twentieth century some people should claim that an ideal for human life is to be found in a society in which the *lex talionis* was in operation at least to some extent. This point deserves to be explained at length. Many Christians think that the principle of 'an eye for an eye' is something inferior, since it has been – to use an Islamic term – 'abrogated' by the teaching of Jesus in the Sermon on the Mount.[21] To think it inferior, however, is in part a misapprehension. In a society where there is no strong ruler with an effective police force the *lex talionis* or retaliation (life for life, eye for eye, etc.) is probably the best way of maintaining a degree of public security. For this reason it is prescribed in both the Old Testament and the Qurʾān.[22] Since there was no central authority capable of punishing a murderer it became the sacred duty of the next of kin to avenge a person's death. The Bible distinguishes between deliberate killing and unintentional killing, and insists that in the former case retaliation *must* be carried out.[23] Even before the revelation of the Qurʾān some Arabs seem to have been substituting a blood-wit (camels or money) for an actual life; but conservative moralists taunted those who accepted camels with being content with milk instead of blood. The Qurʾān encourages the remission of the full penalty and the acceptance of a blood-wit. The general character of life at this time is illustrated by the fact that, when some Muslims were captured by a pagan tribe, they were sold to Meccan families so that they could be put to death in cold blood in retaliation for a member of the family killed in battle with the Muslims. The carrying out of retaliation normally assumed the solidarity of the kin-group.

The basic reason why 'private' retaliation, despite its being prescribed in the Qur'ān, cannot be accepted as an ideal for human society today is not that it is immoral in itself, but that it belongs to, and presupposes, a more primitive structuring of society. In our more civilized and more organized modern societies we have effective police forces and judiciaries, which in most cases are capable of arresting murderers, bringing them to trial and punishing them. Our societies therefore rightly forbid 'private' retaliation, or individuals 'taking the law into their own hands', since there is always the danger that the avenger will exact more than like for like. The Qur'ān, too, insists that the retaliation should be no more than the injury suffered. In pre-Islamic Arabia on one occasion, when a great chief was killed and a young man of the murderer's tribe killed in retaliation, the chief's tribe maintained that this victim counted for no more than a chief's shoe-latchet; and this led to a bloody war. These observations leave open the possibility that there may be a valid principle implicit in the Qur'ānic prescription of retaliation but such a principle can only be applied in modern circumstances if it is admitted that there has been a development in the structuring of human society and that this excludes any right or duty of 'private' retaliation.

Apart from the particular dangers inherent in the idealization of early Islam there is a general danger, namely, that the community becomes so obsessed with recreating something past that it fails to see and deal with the real challenges and problems of the present. Arnold Toynbee in his *Study of History* spoke of the idolization (not idealization) of an ephemeral self or institution, and gave several illustrations at some length.[24] Though he does not mention contemporary Islam, his conception might be applied to it. As has already been suggested, what has been idolized is not early Islam as it actually was, but the self-image of Islam created by the religious scholars in the subsequent three or four centuries. With this image was bound up a structuring of Islamic society based on the elaboration of the Sharīʿa and the formation of a religious institution, which partly worked with the political leadership but was partly independent of it. The creation of the Islamic world community, as it existed from 1000 or earlier until about 1600, is a remarkable achievement, to be reckoned among the finest achievements of humanity as a whole. The inhabitants of a vast area of the world's surface were given a high degree of social stability, which was not seriously disturbed by great political upheavals. Despite this success, however, any attempt to recreate a community based on the same image of early Islam is unlikely to have satisfactory results. What is required is a deeper appreciation of the essential principles implicit in Qur'ān and Ḥadīth, so that solutions to contemporary problems may be found which grow naturally out of the fundamental experiences of the earliest Islam.

This critique of the idealization of early Islam is intended to leave open the possibility that Muslims of today may by meditating on the Qur'ān and the Sīra find inspiration to deal with contemporary problems. To emphasize this point and to suggest more profitable ways of 'going back' to the past, it may be helpful to give a statement about Christianity by two prominent Christian leaders:

> Everywhere throughout the Christian world, as if led by the Spirit, Christians are going back to their roots again. It is not 'Primitivism', the conviction that to find the authentic church we must go back to the first century . . . and then childishly try to recreate some romantic illusion of what seems an ideal age. Rather it is as if the thought of these first ages and their priorities helps Christians to sort out, in the light of many new insights from other disciplines, the elements of their denominational stances that are of lasting relevance and those which are ephemeral and stultifying.[25]

Chapter Two

THE RELIGIOUS INSTITUTION AND ITS DECLINE

The standard Islamic world-view and self-image described in the last chapter were formed over a period of centuries by the religious institution. By the efforts of this institution that world-view came to dominate the thoughts of all Muslims, and the institution is still trying to maintain this dominance. Since this is fundamental to many of the conflicts within the Islamic world today, it is important to look at the present position and attitudes of the religious institution and at sufficient of its past history to make the present comprehensible. The religious institution consists of those who are now commonly called 'clergy' by Western journalists, though they are neither priests nor pastors, but primarily jurists or lawyers. Jurisprudence is and always has been the core of Islamic higher education. Theology, when it is studied, is, as it were, a subordinate subject. The commonest term for these men among Sunnite Muslims is *ʿulamāʾ* (anglicized as 'ulema'), though there are also other terms such as 'mullah'; and 'religious scholars' is a rough translation. In most Islamic countries the ulema fulfil many different functions: judges in Sharīʿa courts, jurisconsults (Muftis), administrators of mosques, preachers in mosques, administrators of *awqāf* (religious trusts), as well as the ordinary work of lawyers.

In the early centuries everything was informal and there was no organization, though there was an understanding or agreement about who was qualified to be an *ʿālim*, one of the ulema. In the Ottoman empire, on the other hand, as will be seen presently, there was an elaborate hierarchical organization, especially in the central provinces; in the Arabic provinces only the senior posts were part of the structure. In these provinces and in most Islamic countries nowadays the body of ulema form a corporation with one of their number as head. Because of the informal relationship between these corporations, it is often convenient to speak of the Sunnite religious institution in the singular. In Iran (which will be described in chapter VI) the situation is quite different, since the official religion is the Imāmite form of Shīʿism.

1 THE RELIGIOUS INSTITUTION AT THE ZENITH OF ITS POWER[1]

In the three centuries or so up to 1850 the religious institution in the Ottoman empire came to be much more highly organized than that in any other part of the Islamic world. It has been suggested that this development may have been due to the fact that the hierarchically-organized Greek Orthodox Church had its main centre in Istanbul. Be that as it may, the religious institution there had at its head a dignitary called the Shaykh al-Islām, who was the third most powerful man in the empire after the Sultan and the Grand Vizier. Under the Shaykh al-Islām the religious scholars were ranged in a number of grades. Membership of these grades depended on academic attainments after attendance at a series of colleges. As men moved up the scale, they were entrusted with lectureships at junior colleges and judgeships in small towns. Many appointments were only for twelve months, and then a man would be moved on, perhaps after an interval, to a position at the next higher level. The whole system of progression was strictly ordered. The highest grades consisted of professorships at the senior colleges and senior judgeships. Apart from this hierarchy of judicial and educational posts there was a looser organization of those with the status of Mufti, that is, those qualified to pronounce a formal legal 'opinion' (*fatwā*). These were appointed for life, but usually received no salary, though they could charge fees for the opinions they gave. The religious institution under the Shaykh al-Islām had thus come to control all higher education, the administration of justice, and, in a sense to be explained, the formulation of laws.

To give an adequate understanding of these points something more must be said about the nature of the Sharīʿa or Islamic law, since it differs in important ways from law as conceived in the West. The Qurʾān contains a relatively small number of legal rules, some of a general character, some more detailed, as in the case of the rules for inheritance. These rules are supplemented by others based on the words or example of Muḥammad as recorded in Ḥadīth. The example of Muḥammad is also referred to as the Sunna. The early religious scholars were men deeply concerned that the administration of the Islamic state and its judicial system should be based on Islamic principles, not on Arab customary usage. They engaged in long oral discussions about what these principles were and how they should be applied in practice; and this became the pattern for legal treatises in later centuries. Much of the discussion was about principles which to the Western observer seem to be ethical rather than legal. Eventually there were many such treatises differing from one another at various points, even if there was a wide area of agreement. The greatest area of consensus was in respect of the practical duties of ordinary people, and these became fairly definite and fixed. Even here, however, there was no single concise formulation of the duties. After the four Sunnite 'schools' (*madhāhib*) came to be recognized, though one could speak of the dominant view within the school on some point, there was still no single authoritative text.

Because the Sharīʿa was of this character, it became important to have persons qualified and authorized to give a legal opinion on *fatwā* on what was right in some novel circumstances. This person was the Mufti. The 'opinion' of a Mufti, however, even when he had an official position, was not final, but could be challenged by another Mufti provided he could counter the arguments of the first Mufti.

The character of the Sharīʿa also affected the functioning of a judge in a Sharīʿa court. Because there was no single authoritative text, he had a degree of flexibility in his decisions, and could introduce slight modifications to meet local conditions, by selecting appropriate texts as a basis. Under the 'Abbāsid caliphate (750–1258) there had come to be other jurisdictions besides that of the Sharīʿa courts. Because of certain weaknesses in the functioning of these courts the caliphs had appointed an official called the *muḥtasib* who had jurisdiction in market affairs and as a censor of public morals. Certain police officers also had been given judicial powers, and in Baghdad a court of superior instance, known as the *maẓālim*, had been instituted to deal with serious civil and criminal cases. The institution of such courts was not contrary to the Sharīʿa, since that left to the ruler a wide discretion in criminal matters. In the Ottoman empire, however, there had come to be some abuse of these jurisdictions, and the sultans had by *ḳanūns* (administrative regulations) and other measures brought them under the ultimate control of the religious institution. This meant that the Shaykh al-Islām and the leading ulema had complete control of the administration of justice, since all the judges in the Sharīʿa courts throughout the empire were members of the religious institution and had been trained in its colleges.

Since jurisprudence was the core of Islamic higher education and since the same persons alternated between being judges and being professors, it is obvious that the religious institution controlled the educational system of the Ottoman empire, and in this way was able to work for the dominance of the traditional world-view and self-image. Education will be dealt with more fully, however, in the fourth section of this chapter.

It is not necessary here to describe further the earlier development of the religious institution,but it is important to say something about its relation to the ruler or more generally, the political institution. During the first century of Islam devout men who wanted to see the Islamic state based on Islamic principles would come together in mosques to discuss such matters. When an individual was recognized as having more than average knowledge and understanding of such questions, he would take up a position in a mosque and lecture to the disciples gathered round him. In the events which led to the replacement of the Umayyad dynasty of caliphs by the ʿAbbāsids in 750 these pious scholars nearly all supported the ʿAbbāsids, and in return they were awarded a degree of official recognition in that judges were mostly appointed from their number.

Recognition of the embryonic religious institution also meant that there were certain political pressures on it. One crisis in the relationship with the ruler was caused by the so-called 'inquisition' (*miḥna*). In 833 (or perhaps earlier) the caliph al-Ma'mūn decreed that the scholars involved in various aspects of legal administration were to make public profession of their belief that the Qur'ān was the created, not the uncreated, word of God. This may seem a pointless theological quibble, but it was linked with a struggle for power between the religious institution and the caliph's 'secretaries' or civil servants. If the Qur'ān is a created word of God, then it might have been created differently, and therefore someone with divine authority (such as was claimed for the caliph by some Muslims) could alter it. On the other hand, if it was uncreated, it expressed something of God's nature and could not be altered; and in this case the final word was with the qualified exponents of the Sharīʿa, the religious scholars, and not with the caliph and his entourage.

Most of the scholars, though believing the opposite, submitted to the demand for a profession of createdness, but one or two refused, notably Aḥmad ibn-Ḥanbal, and were forced into retirement. The 'inquisition' continued intermittently under the next two caliphs, but soon after the accession of al-Mutawakkil in 847 it was abandoned. The political institution had hoped that the doctrine of createdness would heal the division between two important bodies of opinion within the empire, corresponding roughly to later Sunnites and Shīʿites; but by 847 it had become clear that the doctrine was not having this effect since it satisfied neither party. The policy of abandoning the 'inquisition' had as its corollary what was tantamount to the acceptance of Sunnism as the official doctrine of the caliphate. Aḥmad ibn-Ḥanbal was restored to favour, and the religious institution was recognized as authoritative in certain spheres; but it was by no means a complete victory for the religious institution, since its ability to stand up to the political institution had been only too obvious.

From this time onwards there may be said to have been an understanding between the Sunnite religious institution and the changing forms of the political institution (following on the loss of political power by the caliphs in 945). The religious institution was allowed to determine the norms of social life within the caliphate through personal, civil and criminal law, but it was not allowed any say in the external policies of the political institution nor even in respect of the relation of the ruler to his subordinates. In return for this degree of recognition the religious institution gave a title of legitimacy to the political institution.

The period of about a century and a half after the advent of the ʿAbbāsids in 750 was a creative period in the elaboration of the Sharīʿa. During this period a number of 'schools' or 'rites' (*madhāhib*) took shape, of which four came to be accepted as official, while the others faded away gradually. They were not merely 'schools' which differed in respect of theory, but also 'rites' which differed in practice; and since each Muslim had to belong to one, this affected him practically in such matters as the details of how his property was to be divided at his death and the details of the formal prayers (*ṣalāt*). The four Sunnite rites are the Ḥanafite, the Mālikite, the Shāfiʿite and the Ḥanbalite, which take their names from their nominal founders: Abū-Ḥanīffa (d.767); Mālik ibn-Anas (d.795); ash-Shāfiʿī (d.820); Aḥmad ibn-Ḥanbal (d.855). The elaboration of the Sharīʿa within these schools and those which disappeared was based on the right of 'personal effort' (*ijtihād*), that is, the right of a qualified scholar to go back to the primary sources and work out from them what he thought Islamic principles involved. In the first half of the tenth century there seems to have been a consensus that the gate or door of *ijtihād* was now closed, so that there could be no more schools/rites, and that in future religious scholars would be required to follow the precedents established in their rite. There is no record of any actual statement to this effect, but, as in so many other points of Islamic law, there seems to have been an informal consensus. It may well be that this position was adopted in order to defend the religious institution and its members against political pressure, since a judge could now say, 'I cannot bend the law as you want, since I am bound to follow precedent.'

2 TOTALITARIAN STRATEGIES OF THE RELIGIOUS INSTITUTION

Without going further into the history of the development of the religious institution we may now look at the ways in which it worked to bring about the domination of all Islamic thinking by the world-view it was propounding. In his autobiographical work *Deliverance from Error* al-Ghazālī reports how Aḥmad ibn-Ḥanbal once reproved a younger scholar al-Muḥāsibī because he had written a book refuting the doctrines of a heretical sect, the Muʿtazilites, but had first given a full (and perhaps objective) account of their doctrines. Ibn-Ḥanbal was afraid that a reader might be attracted by Muʿtazilite doctrines and accept them without reading the refutation. This attitude is typical of much of the later religious institution. It argued against heresies, but at the same time it tried to prevent any sympathetic presentation of their views from reaching the general body of Muslims. In the works of mainstream Sunnite theology one usually finds that they discuss and refute in detail the views of an earlier generation of heretics, but do not discuss the views of contemporaries. In this way views adjudged heretical could be squeezed out by being given no publicity.

In the tenth and eleventh centuries the theologians, including the practitioners of Kalām who might have been expected to be interested in philosophy, attempted to deal with the Falāsifa or Arabic Neoplatonists in this way by cold-shouldering them. Their works were neither read nor discussed by the theologians. Towards the year 1100, however, one or two men realized that this strategy was not wholly successful, and that the Falāsifa were gaining some support from intelligent people outside the circle of religious scholars. In this situation al-Ghazālī decided that it was desirable that there should be a demonstration of the heretical character of some of their views from the standpoint of theology. He obtained copies of their books, especially those of Ibn-Sīnā (Avicenna), and studied them carefully. He produced a summary of their views, *The Aims of the Falāsifa*, which in some ways is more lucid than their own writings, and then wrote *The Inconsistency of the Falāsifa*, a refutation of those points which he regarded as constituting unbelief or heresy. Philosophy, as a distinct discipline with its own adepts, had been declining in the heartlands of Islam and now disappeared altogether. It continued for a century in the Islamic West and then disappeared there also. Only in the Iranian region did a form of philosophy maintain itself, though one more akin to theosophy. Certain branches of Greek philosophy, notably Aristotelian logic, were retained within the discipline of Kalām. In this way the strategies of the religious institution led to the complete removal of the threat from the Falāsifa. There is a parallel between the medieval treatment of the Falāsifa and the neglect of modern Western thought by Ottoman ulema during the last few centuries. Had the Ottomans conquered Western Europe, the outcome might have been similar; but as things are it is very different.

During the medieval period and up to the present century Muslims have written refutations of Christian teaching, but, in accordance with the point made by Aḥmad ibn-Ḥanbal, they gave only the briefest exposition of Christian beliefs. Moreover because of the doctrine of the 'corruption' of the Bible, Muslims did not engage in discussion with Christians or Jews and had virtually no opportunities of discovering what they really believed, usually remaining content with the Qur'ānic presentation of these religions. It is only within the last decade or two that comparative religion has become a subject of study even in the modern universities of Islamic countries, and so far it does not seem to have made much progress. Apart from the image of Islam as containing all necessary knowledge for living, the study of other religions is discouraged by the Qur'ān in verses (16.106; 88.23f.) prescribing punishments for Muslims who give up Islam for another religion; it was generally maintained in the past by the religious institution that the appropriate punishment was death. This is despite the Qur'ānic statement that there is no compulsion in religion (2.256).

In the present century disciplinary measures have been taken by the religious institution to maintain the traditional world-view and self-image and to thwart attempts to change them. A notable case was that of the Egyptian scholar ʿAlī ʿAbd-ar-Rāziq, a judge in Alexandria and lecturer in the Mosque School there. After the abolition of the caliphate by the Turkish Republic in 1924 and while its future was still being discussed, he wrote a book *Islām wa-uṣūl al-ḥukm* ('Islam and the Principles of Government'), in which he argued that there should be no caliph in the Islamic community on the ground that Muḥammad's power had been essentially religious and spiritual and not political. The book immediately raised a storm of protest, and several books were published defending the contrary view. A court consisting of twenty-five senior ulema from al-Azhar university found him guilty of heresy and of conduct 'unbecoming the character of a religious scholar', and deprived him of his academic qualifications so that he could no longer lecture or function as a judge. He left Egypt and settled in Paris.[2] The essential reason for this bitter attack on an individual appears to have been that he had denied one of the fundamental points of the traditional world-view, namely, that in Islam religion and politics are inseparable – a matter which will be discussed further in chapter V.

In 1926 another book was published which raised a considerable storm. This was a work on 'Pre-Islamic Poetry' (*Fī sh-shiʿr al-jāhilī*) by Ṭāhā Ḥusayn. Using Western methods of literary criticism the author maintained that most pre-Islamic Arabic poetry was a later fabrication; in this he showed himself even more sceptical than most European critics of this poetry, and certainly went too far. Although the authenticity of pre-Islamic poetry cannot be said to be an essential part of the standard Islamic world-view, the religious institution attacked him, probably because it felt that the implicit approval of Western critical methods was dangerous. In the end the book had to be withdrawn, but Ṭāhā Ḥusayn was supported by his colleagues in the Egyptian University (a Western-type institution) on the grounds that academic freedom was being threatened. In 1929 he became the first Egyptian Dean of the Faculty of Arts, then after many ups and downs was Minister of Education from 1950 to 1952. He never recanted his views about pre-Islamic poetry, but when the book was reissued in 1927 under the title 'Pre-Islamic Arab Literature' (changing *shiʿr* to *adab*) he removed the passages in which he had applied the term 'myths' to Qurʾānic stories about Abraham and Ishmael.[3]

The most recent example of this policy of stifling anything at variance with the dominant world-view comes from Pakistan where in 1986 a law was passed prescribing severe penalties for those who wrote or spoke disrespectfully about the prophet Muḥammad. This law seems to have been used to prevent the application of modern historical criticism to any aspect of his career. Pakistan has also passed a number of measures against the modern sect of the Ahmadiyya (to be described in a later chapter). The Ahmadis were finally declared to be non-Muslims and were forbidden to use specifically Muslim words like 'mosque' and 'call to prayer'.

Finally one may note how the attitudes of the religious institution have led to an impoverishment of the Arabic language. Because of the general unconcern with what lies beyond Islam, or perhaps even from a studied neglect of it, the religious scholars paid no attention to European and Christian thought in the modern period (from the sixteenth century). There has been no creative writing in Arabic on the questions raised by Cartesian and post-Cartesian philosophy or by sociological theorists. The result is that it is now impossible to translate many European works into Arabic, because Arabic lacks an adequate vocabulary that is sufficiently precise and definite. Since the nineteenth century, of course, individual Muslims have studied Western thought in the original languages, and have written books in these languages; but these were persons of a liberal outlook. It was said that up until about 1950 none of the professors at the university of al-Azhar read books in any European language. The deficiencies in Arabic created a further barrier for the masses of Arabic-speaking Muslims to prevent them moving beyond the traditional world-view.

3 THE LOSS OF LEGISLATIVE AND JUDICIAL RESPONSIBILITIES

While in the centuries up to about 1850 the religious institution of the Ottoman empire in its central provinces had been growing in power and becoming more highly organized, after 1850 its power rapidly dwindled away. Apart from the general decline of power of the empire, this was the result of the widening gulf between the religious institution and the statesmen, coupled with corruption in the institution itself.

The Ottomans established themselves in south-east Europe in the later fourteenth century, several decades before they gave the final *coup de grâce* to the Byzantine empire by the capture of Constantinople in 1453. The early sixteenth century saw a prodigious expansion of the Ottoman empire, and by the middle of that century it ruled over Yugoslavia, Romania, most of Hungary, the north coasts of the Black Sea to beyond the Sea of Azov, as well as Syria, Iraq, Egypt, the Hejaz and most of North Africa. It was the expansion into Europe, however, which fired the imagination of the Ottoman state:

> its leaders and armies had been march-warriors in the Holy War, carrying the sword and the faith of Islam into new lands. The Ottoman gazis and dervishes, like the pioneers and missionaries of the Americas, believed themselves to be bringing civilization and the true faith to peoples sunk in barbarism and unbelief. . . . For the Ottoman state, the frontier had provided work and recompense both for its men of the sword and its men of religion and, in a deeper sense, the very *raison d'être* of its statehood. . . . The Ottoman systems of military organization, civil administration, taxation, and land tenures were all geared to the needs of a society expanding by conquest and colonization into the lands of the infidel.[4]

In 1529 the Ottoman armies were able to threaten Vienna, and, though they then withdrew, they continued to struggle with Austria for the possession of Hungary and in 1683 again threatened Vienna. Before the end of the sixteenth century, however, the balance of power had begun to shift from the Ottoman side to the Austrian. In the treaty made in 1606 the Ottoman sultan had for the first time to treat with the Austrian emperor as an equal. After the

Ottoman failure at Vienna in 1683 the Austrians advanced rapidly into Hungary, Greece and the Black Sea coast; and in 1699 the Ottomans signed the treaty of Carlovitz as the defeated party and made extensive cessions of territory. In the eighteenth century there were further Ottoman defeats and further cessions of territory, culminating in the treaty of Kuchuk Kaynarja in 1774. From early in the eighteenth century the Ottoman political institution was aware of its decline compared with the Europeans and took some steps to remedy this state of affairs, though little of any significance was achieved. While there was thus a growing awareness within the political institution that reforms were necessary, the will to bring about reforms was for long weakened by the inherited belief in the superiority and self-sufficiency of Islam. This influenced the religious institution to an even greater extent. There were, of course, many factors contributing to Ottoman weakness, such as economic and agricultural decline. The empire was also technologically backward. Though it took over firearms and artillery from the Europeans in the fifteenth century and also European techniques of naval construction and warfare, other changes were slow in being achieved. Jewish and Christian inhabitants of the empire had printing presses from the early sixteenth century, but printing in Turkish and Arabic was forbidden because of pressure from the religious institution and was not finally achieved until 1784 (although a few books were printed between 1729 and 1742).

One result of the general Ottoman weakness was the appearance of corruption in the religious institution, as indeed there was also in the ruling institution and among the Janissaries. Because of the economic decline stipends were worth less, and men were tempted to make up for this in various ways. In particular, those in the higher grades of the religious institution tried to make provision for sons and other relatives. Diplomas were granted which made such persons eligible for many of the higher offices, despite the fact that they did not possess the necessary academic qualifications and had not passed the appropriate examinations. The highest grades of the religious institution thus became a kind of privileged aristocracy, but one without the real learning of previous generations. They were singularly badly equipped for advising the statesmen, since they were more interested in maintaining their own power than in promoting the welfare of the empire as a whole. This is exemplified by their opposition to the introduction of printing. Before the end of the eighteenth century reforming spirits within the ruling institution were aware that the religious institution would resist most reforms; but it was not until nearly the middle of the nineteenth century that effective steps were taken against it.

The real initiation of reform in the Ottoman empire was the work of Sultan Maḥmūd II (1808–39). Up to this period Ottoman statesmen had tended to increase the power of the religious institution by abolishing various previously existing jurisdictions or placing them under the control of the ulema. In 1838, however, Maḥmūd II established a Council of Judicial Ordinances (or Council of Justice), and this was given further powers in 1840. It could not merely supervise the administration of justice, but had also what amounted to legislative powers. Two months later a new penal code was promulgated with the name Kanun-i Ceraim. It had always been accepted that the Sultans could issue Kanuns, which were supposedly no more than administrative regulations, though they sometimes came near to being laws, or at least codifications of laws. This penal code broke new ground in some ways. Though it was mainly in accordance with the Sharīʿa, it also incorporated some French legal ideas; and it was produced by a special group of people, and not according to the normal procedures of the religious institution. Indeed the idea of a code of law was rather foreign to traditional Islamic thinking (as explained above).

Another step forward was taken in 1847 by the creation of 'mixed courts' to hear cases involving Ottoman subjects and non-Ottomans. Hitherto there had been complaints from Europeans doing business with the Ottoman empire because the Sharīʿa courts did not accept evidence from non-Muslims. In the 'mixed courts' there were European and Islamic judges in equal numbers, and the rules of evidence and procedure were more in accordance with European than Islamic practice. In 1850 there followed the promulgation of a Commercial Code, to be administered by commercial tribunals. This was supposedly a Kanun, but was in fact a system of law and judicature outside the scope of the Sharīʿa and not under the control of the religious institution. In 1858 a land code and new penal code were promulgated, and in 1861 and 1863 a further commercial code and a maritime code. In 1860 the 'mixed courts' were amalgamated with the commercial tribunals. Between 1869 and 1876 a document was produced known as the *Mejelle* (in Turkish *Mecelle*) which was a digest or codification of the Sharīʿa in its Ḥanafite form in respect of civil matters, including property and debt. This was in part intended for the guidance in civil matters of those judges who had not had a traditional training in the Sharīʿa. After 1876 there was little further reform until the establishment of the Turkish Republic in 1923.

All this meant that much of the legal and judicial activity in the central provinces of the Ottoman empire was removed from the scope of the Sharīʿa, and was being carried out in courts in which those with a traditional legal training were unable to function. There were still, of course, Sharīʿa courts for matters of personal law – marriage, divorce and inheritance. Under the Republic, however, president Mustafa Kemal, a thoroughgoing reformist, had been only a few months in office when the Sharīʿa courts were closed and replaced by 'independent courts'. At the same time the office of the Shaykh al-Islam was abolished and the ministries for Evkaf (religious trusts) and for the Sharīʿa. The Assembly affirmed that it itself was the supreme legislative power, and in 1926 produced a new legal code based mainly on the Swiss. Since the traditional religious schools were also closed, the religious institution was virtually abolished, or at least its members were left with hardly any functions except leading prayers and preaching in the mosques.

In the Arabic provinces of the Ottoman empire the religious institution suffered severely in the nineteenth century, but still retained some legal and judicial responsibilities. Egypt was nominally a province of the Ottoman empire until 1914, but in 1805 Muḥammad ʿAlī, an Ottoman general of Albanian origin, seized power and was eventually recognized as hereditary Pasha before his death in 1848. The country was then ruled by his descendants until 1952, except that from 1882 until 1922 there was a British occupying force and the chief power was in the hands of the British Resident. In 1874 Egypt became judicially independent of Istanbul, and in 1875 'mixed courts' were established, for which there was a new Civil Code and Penal Code, only partly based on the Sharīʿa and mainly following French models. In 1883 for the 'national courts' there was a similar Civil Code. The Sharīʿa courts still continued, however, and administered personal law and the religious trusts (*awqāf*), but even in their cases some changes were made. After Egypt became independent in 1922 various new laws were passed, not all of which were based on the Sharīʿa. In 1949 both the 'mixed courts' and the Sharīʿa courts were abolished, and instead there were unified 'national courts', though some ulema became judges in the latter.

Something similar occurred in the other Arab countries. In most the traditional religious institution of the ulema continued to deal with personal law in the Sharīʿa courts, but in nearly all there were also other courts and, especially after independence, new laws. The country with fewest changes was Saʿudi Arabia, which for long retained most of the Sharīʿa in its Ḥanbalite form. Even here, however, it was eventually found necessary to have commercial courts or tribunals (using the Ottoman Commercial Code of 1880), and to relax the Sharīʿa in a number of ways. All this meant, of course, that the religious institution in Saʿudi Arabia retained more of its former functions than in other countries. Pakistan tends to be similar to countries like Egypt, but is probably more committed to democratic ideas on the British pattern. Although in 1962 it was declared to be 'a democratic state based on Islamic principles of social justice' and in the following year an 'Islamic Republic', the statesmen have never yielded to the full demands of the ulema for control over all legislation. The recent restoration by General Zia of traditional Islamic penalties, such as the amputation of a hand for theft in certain cases, seems to be a concession made at a time of weakness to get support from the ulema, and does not seem to imply a full acceptance of their demands.

In the last century and a half, then, the religious institution has lost much of its power. Except in the Turkish Republic this has not come about because of any actions reducing or abolishing the power of the ulema, but by the creation of new institutions which gradually took over much of the legal and judicial work formerly carried out by them. This may be said to have been a result of the breakdown of understanding between the religious institution and the ruling groups. The latter were more fully aware of the needs of their countries in the new world that was being created by modern technological, economic and political developments, and saw that reforms and changes were urgent. The religious institution, perhaps because it saw that almost any changes would reduce its power, showed itself obstructive at many points; but the result of this was that the statesmen, as it were, bypassed the ulema. Had the latter co-operated more with the governments than they have in fact done, they might have retained more of their powers. (All this applies only to the Sunnite ulema, since the position of the religious institution in Shī'ite Iran is now quite different.)

4 CHANGES IN EDUCATION

In the field of education much the same happened as in that of law, but the resistance was less. When one of the Ottoman reformers first proposed a commercial code, the ulema objected on the grounds that this was infringing the Sharīʿa; and when the reformer retorted that the Sharīʿa had nothing to do with such matters, he was accused of blasphemy and the proposal had to be dropped.[5] In education, on the other hand, the reformers wanted the teaching of new subjects which the ulema had no desire to teach. One of the first effective schemes was in Egypt. After coming to power in 1805 Muḥammad ʿAlī set about creating an army on the European model; and for this he realized that he required officers with a training in various European subjects not included in the traditional Islamic curriculum, such as forms of mathematics for military engineers. European teachers were therefore brought to Egypt to instruct potential officers; and in 1826 the policy was inaugurated of sending young Egyptians to study in Europe.

In Istanbul naval and military engineering schools had been established before the end of the eighteenth century, but with very limited success. Maḥmūd II followed the initiatives of Muḥammad ʿAlī in Egypt, revived the engineering schools, and began to send students to Europe. He also set up a medical school, with a preparatory section to give primary and secondary education of a Western type; this school aimed at training doctors for the army. In 1834 a School of Military Sciences was opened, and before Maḥmūd's death in 1839 there were two schools for civilians offering education of a Western type. Elaborate plans were made for a complete new system of education up to university level, but the implementation of these plans only came very slowly. A notable advance was the establishment of the Imperial Ottoman Lycée at Galatasaray in 1868, in which the medium of instruction for most subjects was French. Most of the leading Ottoman administrators and diplomats in the later nineteenth century had been to this school. The activity of the politicians in education was stimulated by the creation of Western-type schools by foreign (Christian) missionary bodies, notably Robert College in 1863 by American Protestants.

While this new form of education was developing, a number of ulema obtained qualifications in the new subjects and came to occupy important posts in the political institution. Most of the ulema, however, continued in their usual ways and simply ignored the new schools at all levels. They possibly regarded these as being 'outside their own realm and, perhaps, as ephemeral, worldly institutions, expedient to the needs of secular life.'[6] While the traditional religious 'sciences' (sing. *ʿilm*, 'knowledge for living') remained the monopoly of their *medreses* or colleges, they did not object to the teaching of modern secular disciplines (*fünun*, sing. *fen*) in the Western-type schools. The only protest was in 1870 when the Darülfünun (in effect a university of the new type) proposed to include some of their 'sciences' in its curriculum. Here they were successful in having it closed within a year or two, and it was not finally established until 1900. Since the majority also took the view that knowledge of an infidel language like French was inappropriate for one of their number, those ulema who wanted to acquire something of Western learning had either to study French secretly or else to make a complete break with the religious institution.

It is not necessary here to describe further the progress of Western-type education in what eventually became the Republic of Turkey and the various independent Arab countries. Everywhere there is now a complete system of education of a Western type, with primary schools, secondary schools and universities. At the same time the traditional Islamic system of education has mostly continued in existence. Its lowest level was the Qur'ān-school (*mekteb* or *kuttāb*) in which boys learnt the Qur'ān by heart and at the same time learnt to read. Then there was the *medrese* (or *madrasa*), college, usually a relatively small affair with one main professor of jurisprudence. There were said to have been 275 in Istanbul in the eighteenth century. The most senior *medreses* were carefully graded, and those ulema who aspired to the highest ranks passed through these in a precise order. In Cairo there was a more comprehensive institution, the university of al-Azhar, with a large number of professors. Though jurisprudence was the core subject, the other traditional religious 'sciences' or disciplines were also taught.

This bifurcation of the educational system led, of course, to a cleavage of outlook within the population. Because the religious institution had ignored and cold-shouldered the new system there was normally no religious teaching in it, since the ulema were unfamiliar with the new teaching methods, and the teachers of the new type had no instruction in Islamic religion. Attempts were made in Turkey in the 1930s to have some up-dated teaching of theology and other aspects of Islam, but these were not very successful. In the last decade or two, however, new-type courses of 'religious instruction' in Islam seem to have been developed in Turkey; and one or two universities elsewhere have introduced courses in comparative religion. In most countries, however, the best educated section of the population is more Western than Islamic in outlook, even if many still think of themselves as Muslims, perhaps as good Muslims. A few, especially of those sent to study in the West, have read much of the anti-religious propaganda to be found there, and have become somewhat agnostic in their attitude. Most of those who have been to a new university, or even to the higher classes in secondary schools, have little understanding of the position of the ulema and little sympathy with it. In some countries the cleavage is perhaps not so extreme as stated here, since there have been various compromises between the ulema and the modernizers.

It should be emphasized that this new type of education is not something which has been imposed on the peoples of the Islamic world by nominally Christian colonialists. At certain points, indeed, Christian missionaries (who were not always tools of their government, but sometimes rather at variance with it) established schools and even universities, like the American Universities in Beirut and Cairo. Essentially, however, as in the Ottoman empire, it was the upper classes of the Muslim peoples who wanted this new form of education. It was the statesmen who first became aware of its necessity, as they realized their inferiority to the Europeans, both militarily and in other ways. As time went on it became clear to them that, if the empire and its various provinces were to be adequately administered in contemporary circumstances, they required a large number of men with this new type of training. The more intelligent sections of the population also quickly realized that this new type of education opened up to them much better career prospects than the traditional education of the *medreses*. By the middle of the twentieth century the number of appointments for which *medrese* training qualified was greatly reduced – in Turkey itself none at all.

The position in the Indian subcontinent was somewhat different.

By 1800 India was in effect being ruled by the British, though technically by the East India Company in alliance with local princes. The British established schools to train men for junior posts in their administration, and to these schools many Hindus sent their children but very few Muslims. Before 1857 the ulema were not exactly anti-British, but they discouraged Muslims from obtaining a Western education. They themselves long opposed the study of the infidel language of English, the acceptance of posts in the civil service, and even fraternizing with the British. One result of this attitude was that there were proportionally far more Hindus than Muslims in the junior administrative posts of the political institution, and this was one of the factors contributing to the great Indian Mutiny of 1857, which was mainly a Muslim affair. After the quelling of the Mutiny there appeared enthusiasts for the acceptance of British culture, like Sir Sayyid Ahmad Khan (1817–98), who in 1877 founded the Muhammadan Anglo-Oriental College, which later became the University of Aligarh. Such developments were opposed by the ulema, who had their centres in the Dār al-ʿUlūm at Deoband and the Nadwat al-ʿUlamāʾ at Lucknow. The ulema thus remained conservative, while an increasing number of Muslims had had a Western-type education at least up to secondary school.

As long ago as 1935 a man who was to become one of the leading Muslim thinkers of the subcontinent, Mawdudi, was aware of how the two parallel systems of education had produced two opposing groups among the more intelligent members of the community. Though essentially conservative, he was not a member of the religious institution, and he criticized the ulema for 'still living in the eighteenth century' and giving youth no effective guidance for participation in the contemporary world. He concluded:

> This explains why everywhere in the Muslim world we find two groups and schools of thought diametrically opposed to, and often at loggerheads with each other. One of these is the standard-bearer of Islamic learning and culture, but is incapable of leading and guiding the Muslims in all spheres of life. The other group is controlling the intellectual, literary and political affairs of the Muslims, but is ignorant of the principles and essential features of Islam, alien to the spirit of Islamic culture, and unaware of the character of the communal

organization of Islam and its social laws. Except for a spark of faith in the recesses of his mind, a Muslim belonging to this latter group does not at all differ from a non-Muslim.[7]

5 THE PRESENT POSITION

In the centuries when the Islamic world was more or less unified, the religious institution created the standard world-view and brought it to a position of dominance in the thinking of Sunnite Muslims. In the earlier part of the nineteenth century it was still in possession of great power in the Ottoman empire (which was a large segment of the Islamic world) and had a fair amount of power elsewhere. Between about 1850 and 1950, however, much of this power was lost, and any increases in power since 1950 seem to have been marginal.

This loss of power came about largely because the ulema were unwilling to make concessions in the areas they controlled – the formulation of laws, the administration of justice, education – in order to deal with what the statesmen saw to be urgent contemporary problems. Without formally reducing the powers of the ulema the statesmen created alternative institutions which gradually took over much of the work previously carried out by the ulema.

In many Islamic countries since independence elected bodies have claimed the right to initiate legislation without being subject to the veto of any committee of ulema. There have been some compromises between the old and the new legal and judicial systems, and this varies from country to country. At one extreme is Turkey where a secular system of law was introduced and the ulema have no powers at all. In Saʿudi Arabia, on the other hand, the law followed is mainly the Ḥanbalite form of the Sharīʿa. Other countries are at various points between these two extremes. Even where they have new laws of personal status, these are roughly in accordance with the Sharīʿa, and thus there is still some work for the traditionally trained ulema.

In education the loss of power by the ulema has been spectacular. All Islamic countries have a Western-type educational system up to university level, and it is in this that most of the best brains of the country receive their education. This is absolutely necessary if the countries are to function in the modern world with a reasonable degree of efficiency. One result of this process has been the creation of a new class of Western-educated people, most of whom do not accept the traditional Islamic world-view. These people are aware that the country cannot be run without them, and sometimes feel that they have an inadequate say in their country's future. The ulema have retained their traditional educational system, but it has shrunk in size and importance, since the great majority of children are in the alternative system.

The corporations of ulema in the various countries are mostly very conservative. Some seem to have learnt little from the history of the last century. Thus in Egypt, when in 1961 an exasperated government imposed a reform law upon the ancient university of al-Azhar, the professors employed such obstructionist tactics that for long the reforms were not in fact carried out.[8] Everywhere, except perhaps in Saʻudi Arabia, the ulema are aware that they now have a position of much less importance than formerly in their community, and not least in the political field. Most are consequently filled with a strong desire to regain something of their power and importance. To achieve this they have encouraged and fostered a reassertion of Islamic fundamentalism among the masses; and even some of the better educated people have for various reasons been swept into this movement. In the last two decades the ulema have not necessarily recovered much of their lost ground, but they have certainly increased the domination of the traditional world-view over the minds of Muslims. At the same time, however, many reformist movements have appeared which base their policies on the traditional world-view, and which often criticize the ulema for their subservience to governments.

Chapter Three

THE BEGINNINGS OF ISLAMIC RESURGENCE

A perceptive student of Islamic affairs has written:

> Since the end of the eighteenth century the problem of the dominant West, whether perceived as Christian, secular or atheist, has been the major preoccupation of thinkers and activists, and indeed of all those Muslims who have tried to work out the relevance of the Quranic message for their generation.[1]

While what is now being spoken of as the Islamic resurgence or revival is mainly to be seen among conservatives, all Muslims have had to respond in one way or another to the total impact of the West on their civilization. Some Muslim propagandists have tried to make out that much of the attack on Islam (as they see the matter) was the work of orientalists and missionaries, acting as agents of some deep-laid colonialist plot. To the Western observer it seems clear that the contribution of orientalists and missionaries was minimal, and that much weightier factors were involved. To try to distinguish these it is desirable to look at the main features of the European and Western impact on the Islamic world. There was, of course, a similar impact on other non-European civilizations, but that does not concern us here.

1 RESPONSES TO THE EUROPEAN IMPACT

Some Muslims today regard the European impact on the Islamic world as beginning with the Crusades. There is a measure of truth in this view, but the main modern impact followed on the transoceanic expansion of Europe which began in the fifteenth century, and was differently motivated. For the Islamic world this effectively began in 1498 when Vasco da Gama opened the route to India by the Cape of Good Hope, and various European nations engaged in trade with East Africa, the Indian subcontinent, the East Indies and the Far East. Despite a long tradition of sea-faring among Muslims none managed to become carriers in this new trade. The techniques involved in transoceanic navigation could presumably have been mastered, so that the Muslim failure to make the trade reciprocal was probably due to a lack of encouragement and backing from their home bases.

Trade led on to political involvement. First there were treaties with local rulers, then European troops were sent to protect the trading stations, then there was further interference, and finally in some areas full-blown colonialism. Even when Islamic countries were not ruled by Europeans, there was usually considerable pressure on them to act as the Europeans wanted. One of the important results of this process was that many parts of the Islamic world became integrated into the global (that is, European or Western) economic system. This eventually came to mean in some cases that they had the function of providing raw materials for Europe and in return received manufactured goods.

In Europe itself, to begin with, it was rather a case of the impact of Islam on the European powers through the advance of the Ottoman empire as far as Hungary. This advance had ceased by 1550, however, and towards the end of the seventeenth century it was the turn of the Europeans to advance as a result of a new superiority in military technology. Meanwhile trade increased between European countries and the Ottoman empire, mainly carried, it would seem, in European ships. Diplomatic relations also increased, and there were a few Ottoman diplomats in European capitals, though not so many as the Europeans in Istanbul. By the end of the eighteenth century the Ottomans had become well aware of their inferiority to the Europeans in many practical matters, and within the ruling institution there were a number of men eager for reform. The European diplomats also kept urging the desirability of reform, since a collapse of the empire would have led to a loss of stability over a wide area, and that would not have been in the interests of the European powers.

It should be noted that until late in the nineteenth century few ordinary Muslims had much contact with Europeans. It was chiefly the statesmen and wealthy merchants who met the relatively small number of Europeans who travelled to Islamic countries. Even in a colonialist situation like British India the British personnel met chiefly Indians of the upper classes. Moreover they adopted some of the local customs, and thus to most Indians appeared as only a kind of variant of their own upper class. Things changed towards the end of the nineteenth century as more of the products of European technology and industry became available. The rulers wanted to 'modernize' their countries; first it was armies and modern weapons of war, then railways, then the amenities of domestic life such as electricity and running water, then automobiles and factory equipment, and finally all the new inventions of the twentieth century. As the Western-educated class grew in numbers and wealth it also wanted to share in Western comforts and luxuries. As early as 1877 the explorer Charles Doughty found matches in a small village in Arabia, while about the same time other Arabian travellers, the Blunts, found a telephone instrument in the ruler's mansion in Ha'il, even though it could not be used since there was no network.[2] By the mid-twentieth century most urban Muslims could not but be aware of the Westernization of much of their daily life.

It is important to insist that, apart from the subordination to colonialist rule, most of this development was wanted by Muslims themselves. It could never have been foisted upon unwilling victims by Western exploiters. It was Muslim rulers who wanted to modernize their countries, as well as personally to enjoy European comforts; and these Muslim rulers did not hesitate to get themselves and their countries involved as debtors in the world financial system – or, if one likes, entangled in the web spun by Western spiders. The rulers were not alone in such desires, however. As time went on, more and more of their subjects also wanted to share in the new material standards of living being developed in the West. For this reason many Muslims wanted Western-type education for their children; and the development of the new system of education described in the last chapter could never have come about but for this strong desire among Muslims.

It should not be overlooked that along with the adoption of many of the externals of Western culture, changes also inevitably took place within Muslim society, such as the appearance of a new 'intermediate class' of people with a Western education. Some individuals and groups, too, were able to take advantage of all the new products coming in from Europe, and became better off, sometimes much better off. Other individuals and groups, not necessarily through any lack of enterprise on their own part, became much worse off. All this led to social discontent of one form or another in most countries, though with many variations in detail. Those responsible for bringing in Western technology failed to realize that it would eventually lead to great social upheavals. Social discontent is undoubtedly an important part of the seed-bed for the Islamic resurgence. The ulema also failed to realize this link between social change and the acceptance of Western technology and, while strenuously keeping aloof from any possibility of being corrupted by Western thought, were perfectly ready to take advantage of Western material culture.

The response to colonialism of Muslims (as of Hindus, Buddhists and others) was to demand independence. The most dramatic achievement of independence was that of the Turkish Republic under Mustafa Kemal. By the time most Islamic states became independent after the Second World War, independence involved membership of the United Nations. This meant that Islamic states became part of the world political system, and that Muslim statesmen came into contact with other statesmen throughout the world. This further meant that the statesmen came to see their countries in a much wider perspective than the ulema, who still thought in terms of the 'sphere of Islam' and perhaps also of the 'sphere of war'.

2 THE EROSION OF THE TRADITIONAL SELF-IMAGE

It has been seen above how the idea of Islamic self-sufficiency led the religious scholars of the Ottoman empire and elsewhere to shut themselves off from the new currents of thought which appeared with men like René Descartes, David Hume and the philosophers of the Enlightenment. When Muslim students came to Europe in the nineteenth century, it was inevitable that they should feel that Islam was being attacked, and perhaps also feel that the arguments against Islam were stronger than those for it. What they could hardly realize was that the same anti-religious arguments were being used against Christianity, and had seriously weakened it, but that Christian religious scholars were gradually finding replies to the anti-religious arguments. The awareness of anti-Islamic elements in

Western thought communicated itself to some extent to ordinary Muslims at home, especially to the Western-educated, and even to the religious scholars. There was still some Christian anti-Islamic polemic which presented Islam in a bad light, but this was much less influential than the general climate of Western thought.

Fundamentalist propagandists today accuse orientalists of being agents of a political master-plan for annihilating Islam. (It is amusing to find Christian missionaries included in this charge in the monthly journal of the Islamic Call Society, a body funded by Colonel Qadhafi, which engages in activities almost identical with those of Christian missionary societies; and it is difficult to see why the first should be very wicked while the agents of the latter are almost angels of light.) It may be admitted that the earliest Christian scholars to study Islam seriously in the twelfth and thirteenth centuries did create what has been called a 'distorted image' of it; but they were doing no more than defending their fellow-Christians by enabling them to feel that, even if the Muslim enemy was militarily and culturally superior to them (as it was), yet they had a superior religion. Later scholars, especially during the last hundred years, have tried hard to correct the distortions. As long ago as 1734 George Sale produced an accurate English translation of the Qur'ān made in accordance with the interpretations of the commentator al-Bayḍāwī, who is generally considered one of the most authoritative.

For the last century or more Western scholars have been guided in their endeavours by the scholarly ideal of objective truth. This, of course, is closely linked with the knowledge for power which was distinguished above from knowledge for living. Objective truth is knowledge of things as they really are, and this is the kind of knowledge which gives people control over things. When modern Muslim propagandists complain that the knowledge gained by orientalists enabled their governments to threaten the destruction of Islam, one is inclined to ask why Muslim scholars did not make a similar study of Europe and Christianity on behalf of their governments. Was their failure to do so due to the faulty image of Islamic self-sufficiency? Actually most orientalists were probably moved as much by curiosity as by anything else. Many were primarily interested in eastern religions, a subject which was not of great value for aggressive colonialist politicians.

What was being attacked by the orientalists and by Western

thought generally was not Islam as such in its essentials, though some Muslims might think this, but some secondary aspects of the traditional Islamic self-image and world-view. These were aspects which were liable to be eroded by the 'acids of modernity' as soon as they were exposed to them. Thus claims to historicity were implicit in the world-view, but some of these claims could not be upheld in the light of the critical methodology which had come to dominate Western historical studies. One of the important fields in which Western scholars were sceptical was that of Ḥadīth, the anecdotes about Muḥammad, where they took the view that many Ḥadīth were not authentic even when accepted as 'sound' by Muslim authorities. Another matter is the belief that Muḥammad's coming as a prophet is exactly foretold in the Bible; this idea is not even seriously considered by Christian scholars nowadays, since they have ceased to believe that God makes precise revelations of this kind about a long-distant future, holding instead that the messages which the Biblical prophets received from God were all primarily for their own time and place. Where prophets described a future messianic age, this was in general terms and without any precise historical reference, being rather a statement of the principles according to which God treats human beings.

In the West many anti-religious trends have, rightly or wrongly, been associated with science, but Christian scholars have now mostly come to terms with these, either by refuting them or by interpreting Christian doctrine in such a way that it does not contradict the assured results of science. Muslims, when first exposed to such trends, find it difficult to know how to respond. The concept of evolution has proved particularly difficult. Christian theologians now mostly accept evolution as a fact, and hold that God creates the world through the evolutionary process. Many Muslims try to avoid admitting that evolution has taken place by claiming that scientists are not agreed about it; but these Muslims fail to realize that what scientists are disputing is a *theory* of how evolution came about, not the *fact* that *Homo sapiens* has evolved from lower forms of life. It is somewhat pathetic to see Muslim traditionalists thus clutching at straws. In somewhat similar vein they have given wide publicity to a book by a French physician, Maurice Boucaille, in which he claims that, while there is much in the Bible contrary to modern science, there is nothing at all in the Qur'ān. Again there is a failure to realize that all such criticisms of the Bible have been dealt with long ago by Christian scholars. If traditionalist Muslims had had a deeper understanding of contemporary Western thought, they would have seen that what appeared to them as attacks on Islam were not the work of any groups deliberately plotting against Islam, but were the inevitable outcome of the exposure of their traditional world-view to the contemporary Western outlook. They might also have come to see that they could not share in Western science and technology without also sharing in those aspects of Western thought on which science and technology are based, and that these could not be wholly separated from the historical and literary criticism which threw doubts on parts of their traditional world-view.

In his book *Jung and the Story of our Time*[3] Laurens van der Post talks about the place of 'stories' in the life of the Bushmen of South Africa: 'I realized that the story was their most precious possession. . . . They knew how dangerous it was to let a foreigner . . . in on the secret of their stories. He might destroy them.' It would seem that in the case of these Bushmen the 'story' is part of what I have been calling the self-image. Others might speak of it as the 'myth' in a positive, not a pejorative, sense or yet again as the 'identity' of a people. It is clear that for Muslims their 'story' is the self-image, either in the form described above or in some other form; and traditionalist ulema are rightly alarmed because they see that Western thought is threatening to destroy it. Because they have no understanding of Western thought, after having shut themselves off from it for centuries, they are unable to defend the self-image by argument in a way that would satisfy Western-educated Muslim youth. As a result all they can do is to reassert the self-image as something unchanging in an unstable world, and to call Muslims to a more adequate observance of the praxis of the earliest Islam.

The alternative response is that of those Muslims who may be called liberals in a very wide sense. Some of these have an excellent understanding of Western thought, and are trying to find ways to transform the Islamic world-view and self-image, so that this can form a basis for their living out their Islamic faith in the late twentieth century. These thinkers will be dealt with in the next chapter. Meanwhile we may look at one or two men who have defended the traditional self-image without altogether withdrawing into a ghetto.

3 CONSERVATIVE REFORMERS AND ACTIVISTS

One or two Muslims, who could be described as conservative in outlook in a general way, have responded to the erosion of the traditional world-view not by a bare reassertion of its validity, but by a wider and more positive response which included a reforming element.

(a) Muḥammad ʿAbduh

The first man of this kind to be noticed here is the Egyptian Muḥammad ʿAbduh (1849–1905). He received a traditional education which was completed at the university of al-Azhar, but he was critical of some aspects of this education. In his twenties he came under the influence of Jamāl-ad-Dīn al-Afghānī (1839–97), a man who travelled in many parts of the Islamic world exhorting Muslims to unite in order to resist the influence of Europe and the West. From 1882 to 1888 Muḥammad ʿAbduh was in exile and spent part of this time in Paris with al-Afghānī. Eventually, however, he became less interested in the latter's political programme and more interested in educational and legal reforms. From 1899 to 1905 he was Grand Mufti of Egypt and had considerable political influence.

There was an important study of Muḥammad ʿAbduh by Charles C. Adams under the title of *Islam and Modernism in Egypt: A Study of the Modern Reform Movement inaugurated by Muḥammad ʿAbduh.*[4] While there is truth in this conception of a modernizing reform movement, Muḥammad ʿAbduh has been placed in a slightly false perspective. The movement he inaugurated was different from those other modernizing movements described as 'liberal' to be considered in the next chapter, since he was essentially a conservative and was not trying to transform the Islamic self-image. He indeed wanted reforms because he was aware of the unsatisfactory conditions in Egypt and other Islamic countries, and saw that these were partly due to the Westernized system of education. At the same time he was aware of the weaknesses in traditional Islamic education at the higher levels, because in his early days this was still concentrating on memorization of texts without much comprehension of their meaning. He wanted the students to obtain a reasoned understanding of the texts, and, while still himself a student at al-Azhar was expounding to fellow-students theological texts which the professors thought too difficult to handle. He also saw the need for extensive legal reforms. The troubles of Egypt and other Islamic countries, however, he did not ascribe wholly to foreign influences, but tended to blame the Muslims themselves for failing to live out Islamic principles adequately; and for this reason he wanted a more effective form of Islamic education. During the last few years of his life he used his power to try to bring about reforms at al-Azhar, but, apart from improving the conditions of professors and students, accomplished little owing to the opposition of the majority of the ulema.

Unlike most of his fellow-ulema he was interested in Western thought, and had some acquaintance with it, both from the time he spent in Europe and from the reading knowledge of French which he acquired when he was over 40. He was by no means an enthusiast for Western thought, however, and part of his ideal for Islamic education, besides the appeal to reason, was the elimination of foreign elements. The most complete account of his views is that in *The Theology of Unity* (*Risālat at-tawḥīd*).[5] This could best be described as a reaffirmation of the traditional Islamic world-view and self-image. The finality and superiority of Islam is emphasized and also its place in world history. His desire to get rid of foreign elements indicates his belief in Islamic self-sufficiency. His presentation of theological doctrine is modernistic in the sense that it avoids traditional theological language, but his use of reason in this presentation is entirely within the Islamic tradition and owes nothing to European thinkers. He does not seem to be concerned with the anti-religious philosophies current in Europe, but he does take notice of the attacks on religion from a scientific standpoint. On this matter he defends the Islamic self-image by holding that, if reason is properly used in investigating created being (that is, in scientific matters), the results it reaches will accord with the divine truth to be learnt from religion. At the same time he claimed that reason had a prominent place within religion, and regarded the pure Islam which he desired as capable of being rationally defended and justified.

Apart from his general references to the critique of religion from a scientific standpoint Muḥammad ʿAbduh shows no awareness of the erosion of the Islamic world-view by Western thought. Ignaz Goldziher's attack on the authenticity of Ḥadīth in his *Muhammedanische Studien* was published in 1890 in German and was probably not known to him, but he shows no knowledge either of earlier accounts of the life of Muḥammad. On the contrary, in the section of his book on 'the Mission and Message of Muḥammad' he rewrites history according to his own imagination in a way that would hardly have been possible if he had had any real appreciation of Western historico-critical methods. In other words the basic reform which Muḥammad 'Abduh is seeking is a more rational understanding and presentation of Islamic truth. Apart from that he is reasserting the traditional self-image. The most one can say is that, but for the general impact of the West on the Islamic world, he might not have felt the need for such a reassertion.

(b) Ḥasan al-Bannā'

Another Egyptian leader was Ḥasan al-Bannā' (1906–49), the founder of the Muslim Brotherhood (Al-Ikhwān al-Muslimūn).[6] His early education was in part a traditional one, since his father, though a watchmaker, was also a Ḥanbalite scholar; but his training as a teacher was at least partly of a Western type and he was qualified to teach in government schools. He was influenced to some extent by the followers of Muḥammad ʿAbduh and agreed in deploring the low level of Islamic praxis among the masses and emphasizing the need to work for a purer Islam. His religious fervour deepened when he became a member of a sufi order. He was always critical of the Westernized élite and 'intermediate class'.

In 1928, after being appointed to a teaching post in Ismailiya, he there founded the Muslim Brotherhood. This came to be organized in small units called 'families' together with larger groupings. While there were social and athletic activities, the main emphasis at first was on religious instruction for Muslim youth, since many had little knowledge of their religion. In this Ḥasan al-Bannā' and his helpers could be regarded as doing something to fill the void caused by the absence of religious teaching in the Western-type schools. A need was certainly being met, for the movement spread rapidly, especially after Ḥasan al-Bannā' was moved to Cairo in 1933. At its greatest extent the Muslim Brotherhood is thought to have had half a million or even a million members and sympathizers. It thus became a mass movement and latterly contained within itself many divergent groups, some more activist than others. It inevitably became involved in politics, though this was not part of its original aims. The history of the political activities of the Brotherhood and of groups associated with it is much too complex to be described here. Political involvement led to Ḥasan al-Bannāʾ himself being assassinated in 1949. Under his successor the Brotherhood supported the Free Officers in 1952 when the king was expelled, but it found the new government too sympathetic to Western ideals and not sufficiently Islamic. In 1954 some of its members were allegedly implicated in a plot to assassinate Gamal Abd-an-Nasser, and its overt activities ceased for a time. It still continues as an important influence in the background of Egyptian politics.

Although from time to time political activists within the Brotherhood or associated with it attracted attention, sometimes adverse, the most important fact about it is probably its contribution to the general movement of Islamic resurgence in Egypt and other countries like Syria, Jordan and the Sudan. At times it has talked about social reforms, though always based on the Sharīʿa. A noteworthy programme of social reform was put forward in a book entitled *Social Justice in Islam* (*Al-ʿAdāla al-ijtimaʿiyya fī l-Islām*) by one of its members, Sayyid Quṭb, who was executed in 1965 for his political activities. Though insisting on a return to the Sharīʿa, the Brotherhood did not want a restoration of medieval punishments, and said, for example, that the amputation of a hand to punish theft was only to be carried out in a perfect Islamic state where there was no want. This reforming side of the Brotherhood had little success since there was insufficient agreement among the members. Gradually the movement has become more conservative, has said little about reform and has become more concerned about the reassertion of the traditional self-image. Despite this conservatism the Brotherhood was critical of the Egyptian ulema, whom it saw as often being unduly subservient to the government, even when the latter's policies were based on Western values, not Islamic.

From the first the Brotherhood insisted that its members should lead upright lives according to Islamic principles. Among the things to be avoided were gambling and sexual unchastity; but as time went on, the emphasis came to be more and more on the points which are distinctive of the Islamic resurgence generally. These are the avoidance of alcoholic beverages, the avoidance of usury (the lending of money for a fixed rate of interest) and the insistence on modest dress for women. The reason why these three points have been singled out is doubtless that they mark off Muslims from most Westerners and thus make their distinctive identity obvious. In Egypt the Brotherhood is said to be particularly strong among students at universities; and among many sections of the population there is probably now considerable social pressure to conform to the Brotherhood position at least outwardly.

(c) Mawdudi

In the Indian subcontinent the career of Mawdudi (Sayyid Abū-l-Aʿlā al-Mawdūdī) (1904–79) is comparable to that of Ḥasan al-Bannāʾ in Egypt. Like the latter Mawdudi was not one of the ulema but primarily a journalist, though he was well instructed in traditional Islamic learning. In 1941 he founded an association, Jamāʿat-i Islāmī, not unlike the Muslim Brotherhood. The main purpose of this was to give young men fuller instruction in the true Islam. Since 1932 Mawdudi had been publishing a religious monthly with a similar aim. Like the Brotherhood, too, the Jamāʿat was involved in politics, and Mawdudi served some prison sentences. Originally he was opposed to the creation of a separate state of Pakistan but, once that had come into existence, he endeavoured to ensure that it would have a truly Islamic character. The Jamāʿat was not so numerous as the Brotherhood, and so its political influence was less.

At the heart of Mawdudi's teaching was a restatement of the traditional world-view and self-image, but this was put in a popular form which could appeal to large numbers of people with a moderate degree of education. An early general presentation is contained in his book *Towards Understanding Islam*,[7] where he has sections entitled a 'rational vindication' of prophethood and of life after death, and further asserts that by 'correct use of his knowledge and intellect' a man will come to know God and Islam.[8] This book emphasizes the finality, superiority and self-sufficiency of Islam (as expounded in chapter 1), but does not touch on its place in history apart from giving a gloomy unhistorical account of the low level of spiritual life in the countries surrounding Arabia in the early seventh century.

Mawdudi is extremely critical of the West which he regards as entirely atheistic and materialistic. It has studied the phenomena of nature, he says, on the assumption that there is nothing in the world beyond what is known to the senses, and so has failed to realize that the world has a Creator and Master. The civilization it has produced is seriously flawed, with the result that 'an endless crop of troubles has sprung from this pernicious tree of civilization and culture, making life hell for the peoples of the West.'[9] He does not blame the West for all the troubles of the Islamic world, but thinks that Muslims themselves are partly to blame:

> Western civilization is of course no match for Islam; indeed, if the conflict had been with Islam as such, no other civilization could possibly have the better of Islam. But the tragedy is that Islam with which Western civilization happens to be in conflict today is a mere shadow of the real Islam. The Muslims are devoid of Islamic character and morals, ideas and ideology, and have lost the Islamic spirit. The true spirit of Islam is neither in their mosques nor schools, neither in their private lives nor in the public affairs. Their practical life has lost all its association with Islam. The Law of Islam does not now govern their private or collective conduct.[10]

Like the Muslim Brotherhood in Egypt Mawdudi sees the ulema as specially to blame for the 'critical revolution' through which the Islamic world is passing:

> Much of the blame for this dangerous situation must be accepted by our leaders of religion. It was their duty, right at the outset of the revolution, to bestir themselves and try to comprehend the principles and essential features of the new civilization of the West, and to go out to the Western lands to study the intellectual and scientific foundations on which the edifice of that civilization was being raised. With the help of *ijtihad* they should have striven to persuade the Muslims to accept and press into service the useful practical knowledge and scientific discoveries that had enabled the Western nations to achieve such remarkable progress. And they should have sought to fit these new instruments of progress, in keeping with the principles of Islam, into the educational system and social life of the Muslims.[11]

The last two sentences here suggest that Mawdudi is in favour of reforms which will lead to a more satisfactory application of the Sharīʿa in today's conditions. At an earlier point in the lecture he had suggested that the Muslims had forfeited their supremacy in a large part of the world because they had 'lost their ability to interpret the *Shariah* in the changing conditions'.[12] Despite this apparently forward-looking approach by Mawdudi to social questions, the actual programme of reform supported by the Jamāʿat was slight. Mawdudi even emphasized that disparity of wealth was part of the divine scheme of things:

> The principle that man should be free to strive for his livelihood, that he should retain the right of ownership over whatever he earns by his labour, and that disparity must exist between various men due to their varying abilities and circumstances has been conceded by Islam to the extent to which it is in accordance with nature.[13]

He also expresses the belief that to prevent undue disparities in wealth all that is necessary is that traditional Islamic laws (about usury, monopolies, speculation and the like) should be observed, but he does not say precisely how this is to be achieved:

> If you study in detail the Islamic laws of trade and industry, you will see that the methods by which people become millionaires and multi-millionaires in modern times are mostly methods on which Islam has placed stringent legal restrictions. If business is carried on within these Islamic limitations, there is little possibility of anyone accumulating immense wealth.[14]

This last assertion seems to have been completely disproved when vast oil reserves were discovered in territories belonging to Muslims. Indeed, it is difficult to resist the conclusion that Mawdudi's remarks were little more than pious aspirations. There was never sufficient elaboration of detail to enable them to become matters of practical politics. The result of this has been that the main achievement of the Jamāʿat in Pakistan has been to strengthen the hold of the traditional world-view and self-image.

(d) Colonel Qadhafi

A brief notice should be given to Colonel Qadhafi of Libya (Muʿammar al-Qadhdhāfī). He has propounded a 'third international theory' and put it into practice in Libya. The theory is intended as a counter to both capitalism and communism. The chief point appears to be that all the people in a village or all the workers in a factory should participate in the decision-making process for the state as a whole by taking part in 'people's conferences' (*muʿtamirāt*), which then report to other higher-level bodies. This seems to be an attempt to extend the idea of the assembly of all the members of a tribe; but it is unlikely to be well received in the vast conurbations of today. More important in the present context is his establishment of the Islamic Call Society to carry on what Christians would term missionary work throughout the world. The word 'call' translates *daʿwa* which is the calling or summoning of people to God; but the use of a different word enables the claim to be made that what Muslims do is very different from what Christians do. With the funds which the Colonel provides, the Society is able to build mosques for Muslim groups in many countries as well as arranging for religious instruction. There is a strong emphasis on politics, but in the properly religious sphere it is the traditional world-view and self-image which are being reaffirmed. The Society also produces a glossy monthly journal, of which the English edition has provided illustrative quotations for the present study. Although Colonel Qadhafi's stance is basically traditional, he also involves some liberal Muslims in the affairs of the Society.

(e) The Ahmadiyya sect

The Ahmadiyya movement is important as showing an unusual Islamic response to the impact of the West, but at the same time one that has been vehemently rejected by the majority of Muslims. The movement came into being in the Punjab in the last two decades of the nineteenth century through the preaching and writing of Mirza Ghulam Ahmad (1836–1908). He adopted the missionary methods both of Christian missionaries and of Hindu and Sikh reformists, and he and his followers have been so successful and so well organized that there are now reckoned to be about 10 million Ahmadis, about 4 million in Pakistan and the rest in various Western and African countries. The original centre was at the village of Qadian, now in India, but after partition was moved to Rabwah in Pakistan. After the death of the first 'successor' (*khalīfa*) of the founder the movement split into two sections, usually known as the Qadianis and Lahoris. Both have mosques in London.

Ghulam Ahmad claimed to be a renewer (*mujaddid*) of Islam and also in some sense a prophet (*nabī*). Later he made further claims to be the Promised Messiah expected by Christians, and also for Hindus an avatar of Krishna. This is obviously a response to the situation of religious pluralism existing in India, and is in contrast to the silence of most Muslims about other religions. As early as 1891 the ulema denounced the views of Ghulam Ahmad as heretical, and opposition still continues both in Pakistan and in some African countries. In 1984 the government of Pakistan declared the Ahmadis to be non-Muslims and forbade them to use Islamic terms such as 'mosque'. The main point objected to was the claim to be a prophet, since according to standard Sunnite doctrine Muḥammad is the last of the prophets; but more worldly considerations were probably also involved. Ghulam Ahmad certainly claimed to be a prophet, but not in the sense of establishing a new religion with a new scripture, only as reinterpreting the Qur'ān. It is noteworthy that the Lahori section, who hold their founder to be a renewer of religion but not a prophet, are also included in the 1984 condemnation.

The main aim of the movement was to recall Muslims to a true Islam, expressed in traditional Qur'ānic terms. Personal piety was emphasized, and much of the success of the movement seems to have been due to its ability to help people to develop a personal devotional life. It fully accepted traditional ideas about purdah for women, but it interpreted *jihād* as a spiritual and not a political and military struggle. In a sense, then, the Ahmadiyya may be said to have accepted a privatized form of religion on the Western model.

The most distinguished member of the Ahmadiyya in recent times has been Sir Muhammad Zafrulla Khan (1893–1985). After a distinguished career as lawyer and administrator before partition, he became Pakistan's first foreign minister (from 1947 to 1954). In 1961 he went to the United Nations as Pakistan's representative, and in the following year was elected President of the General Assembly. He was also associated with the International Court of Justice at the Hague, and from 1970 to 1973 was its president. Of his numerous books and pamphlets two may be mentioned. *Muhammad, Seal of the Prophets*[15] contains, to the best of my knowledge, nothing to which any Sunnite Muslim could object. An earlier work, *Islam, its Meaning for Modern Man*,[16] is one of the best presentations of Islam to Westerners by a Muslim. He has one paragraph about the founder of the Ahmadiyya Movement, in which, in order to show the relevance of the Qur'ān to contemporary problems, he quotes a passage of the Qur'ān (62.3f.) and gives a non-Sunnite interpretation:

> This means a spiritual second advent of the Prophet for the purpose of setting forth from the Quran guidance that may be needed in the New Age, and for illustrating the values demanded by the exigencies with which man may then be faced. This promise has been fulfilled in the advent of Ahmad of Qadian.[17]

He also has a couple of pages with a factual account of the missionary work of the Ahmadiyya Movement, and describes its aim as follows:

> The purpose of the Movement is to revive Islamic values derived from the Quran and the example of the Prophet, in every sphere of life, and to carry far and wide the message of Islam, with particular emphasis on its application to the present age.

The rest of the book, so far as I have noticed, has nothing at variance with Sunnite teaching. Indeed Zafrulla Khan moves away from the privatized religion of Ghulam Ahmad, and, as one might expect from a man with his experience as a statesman, has sections on public affairs and international relations. Although this exposition of Islam is in a modern idiom, adapted to the Western outlook, it is very much in accordance with the traditional worldview.[18]

While at first sight the traditionalists' attack on Mirza Ghulam Ahmad's claim to be a prophet does not seem to be altogether justified, yet closer examination shows that implicit in his treatment of the Qur'ān was a claim to be able to reinterpret it by a kind of inspiration and without reference to the traditional interpretations and to the methods of the ulema; and this was a sapping of the foundations of the religious institution. The treatment of the Ahmadiyya in Pakistan gives one some idea of the virulent opposition any future *mujaddid* will have to meet.

(f) Concluding remark

As one reviews the movements described here it seems clear that these, perhaps with the exception of the Ahmadiyya, have made a contribution of first importance to the Islamic resurgence, and that this has been more effective than the attempts at reform in which some members engaged from time to time. The chief exception is possibly that in the field of traditional education there has been some improvement in the method of teaching, though hardly anything amounting to a real reform, such as changes in the curriculum would be. Perhaps the criticisms of the ulema by these movements have had some effect. The ulema have, of course, continued to affirm the traditional world-view, and have tried to use the support they received from the resurgence to obtain changes they wanted to see, such as a return to some medieval interpretations of the Sharīʿa.

The fundamental reason for the resurgence appears to be the feeling among many ordinary Muslims, including some of the better educated, that they were in danger of losing their identity – what Laurens van der Post called their 'story' – because of its erosion by Western intellectual attitudes. At the same time many of these people felt that in the social upheaval caused by the impact of the West on their world they were faring rather worse than many other groups; and many traditionalists were promising that a return to the true Islam of the earliest period would solve all social problems.

Chapter Four

THE LIBERAL SEARCH FOR A NEW IDENTITY

The term 'liberal' is being used in this book, as already explained, to indicate those Muslims who appreciated much of the Western outlook and felt that the implicit or explicit criticisms of Islam were partly justified, but who at the same time thought of themselves as Muslims and wanted to live their lives as Muslims. While conservatives tried to meet the threat to Muslim identity by admitting weaknesses in existing Islamic praxis and calling for a return to a more genuine Islam, that is, to a more complete living out of the traditional identity, the liberals began to look for a new identity which, in some respects at least, would be more in accord with Western values.

1 THE EARLY LIBERALS

Various studies are available of the liberal movements in Islam prior to the achievement of independence by most Muslim countries between 1945 and 1962. It is not necessary in the present context to attempt to describe all the social and political reforms suggested by liberal Muslims. Attention will be focused on what is relevant to the elaboration of a new identity or self-image.

The development of liberal thought in Indian Islam was covered in detail by Wilfred Cantwell Smith in his *Modern Islam in India.*[1] Sir Hamilton Gibb in his Haskell lectures on *Modern Trends in Islam*[2] described the Arab world and Turkey as well as the subcontinent, and provided an analysis of the general character of Islamic modernism. Kenneth Cragg in his *Counsels in Contemporary Islam*[3] dealt with the same area but was also able to include some of the later post-independence movements.

A convenient starting-point is Sir Hamilton Gibb's critique of those he calls 'modernists' but who are roughly the same as those here described as liberals. He notes that in the period with which he was concerned (up to 1945) they had accepted certain aspects of the Western outlook but not others. He considered that what had influenced them most was the romanticism which had been prominent in the Western outlook in the nineteenth century when Muslims first began to come in contact with it. By romanticism he meant an emphasis on the imaginative and feeling elements in culture as contrasted with the 'classical' and rational. With romanticism he associated the nationalism which emphasized the values incorporated in national history. Along with romanticism among Muslims went a disregard of Western historical criticism. Although some of the most devastating critiques of the traditional self-image came from Western historical criticism, the modernists or liberals were content to reply to these critiques by such measures as an idealization of Muḥammad which was largely unhistorical. More recently they have insisted with some slight justification that modern Western science is derived from medieval Islamic science.

While what Gibb says about the adverse effects of romanticism is largely correct, there is also a positive side which he rather neglects. Nationalism gives people a sense of identity as members of a nation which has incorporated certain values in its past history. When he says that modernizing Muslims have adopted a 'nationalistic interpretation of Islam, going back to Jamāl-ad-Dīn al-Afghānī' (p.111), that seems to mean no more than that they saw the Islamic community as incorporating certain values in its history; and this presentation of history is justified provided the particular assertions are sound. Gibb may have felt, of course, that many of the particular assertions were unhistorical.

These points may be illustrated from the movement in the subcontinent associated with Sir Sayyid Ahmad Khan and Ameer Ali. After the disastrous defeat of the Muslims in the Indian Mutiny in 1857 and the consequent attitude of dejection, Sayyid Ahmad Khan (1817–98) set about trying to raise their spirits by persuading them to adopt a policy of co-operation with the British. This involved a degree of acceptance of Western values, since it implied that Muslim boys would attend the schools established in order to train them for government service. One of Sayyid Ahmad Khan's achievements was the opening in 1877 of the college which in 1920 became the University of Aligarh. The best known work to come out of this movement is *The Spirit of Islam* by Ameer Ali (Sayyid Amīr ʿAlī, 1849–1928).[4] The book was essentially a presentation of Islam and its founder as embodying all the liberal values admired in Victorian England. Ameer Ali saw Muḥammad as a 'great Teacher', a believer in progress, an upholder of the use of reason and indeed 'the great Pioneer of Rationalism', in short as a thoroughly modern man. Islam he regarded as in every way an ideal religion, inculcating a true belief in God and insisting on moral purity and a high ethical code. Its wars were purely defensive. It raised the status of women. It improved the lot of slaves and discouraged slavery. It encouraged learning and science, and emphasized human responsibility and the freedom of the will. Evidence was given for these assertions, and contrary views were argued against.

The Spirit of Islam has been translated into several Islamic languages, and has exercised a wide influence over the outlook of Western-educated Muslims. In place of the traditionalist image of Islam it has given them a new image which enables them to feel that as Muslims they have an identity at least as good as that of Westerners. What is so meaningful for the Western-educated, however, is meaningless for the mass of ordinary Muslims.

Speaking in 1945 Sir Hamilton Gibb saw clearly that up to that date the liberals had been ineffective in bringing about any significant change in Muslim opinion in general. One reason for this was 'their failure to grasp the fact that no endeavour can succeed unless it achieves a balance between the broad and deep currents of a people's psychology and the inescapable forces of social evolution' (p. 113), or, as we might say, between a people's deep attachment to their self-image and the consequences of being part of the twentieth-century world. Gibb noted various alternatives open to the modernists after the abolition of the caliphate in 1924: the setting-up of a purely spiritual caliphate; the building of separate Muslim nation-states; and the 'violent assertion of the supremacy of the sacred law' or Mahdism, as he sometimes called it; and he argued that none of these alternatives held out much hope for the future of Islam.

Another weakness of the modernists was, as has already been mentioned, their 'disregard of historical thinking'. For one thing this led them to exaggerate the social successes of Islam in the past and the social evils found in the contemporary West. More seriously, however, it meant that they were providing responses to existing situations which were imaginatively and emotionally satisfying, but which kept people from appreciating the fundamental problems. He particularly notes that the modernists had 'not yet formulated to themselves a coherent social ideal adapted to the needs of Muslims generally' (p. 111). In his closing pages he suggests that one of the greatest needs of Muslims is to cultivate historical thinking and so become better able to evaluate 'the data of thought' and to move towards 'freeing the vision of the great overriding movement of the Eternal Reason from the frailties, the halting interpretations and the fussy embroideries of its human instruments and agents' (pp. 126–7).

2 CONTEMPORARY LIBERAL THINKING

Turkey achieved its independence in 1922, and some of the Arab countries had a measure of independence from about that period, but the latter and the other main Islamic countries only obtained full independence in the years between 1945 and 1962. For present purposes it will be convenient to regard as contemporary the happenings of the last quarter of a century or so.

The dominant feature of this period has, of course, been the Islamic resurgence, along with an increase in the strength and influence of the conservative elements. This has meant increasing pressure on the liberals in most Islamic countries, making it difficult for them to disseminate their views freely. Some Islamic governments, such as that of Pakistan, have, perhaps because of weakness, acceded to certain demands of the conservative ulema; examples of this have been given earlier.

Of all the predominantly Islamic countries it is probably in Turkey that the liberals have been most successful.[5] There was an abortive attempt in 1924 to set up a liberal faculty of theology in the University of Istanbul. In 1949 a faculty of theology was actually established in Ankara University, and this has gradually overcome the many obstacles encountered, such as the finding of suitable teachers. In 1971 a faculty of Islamic studies was set up in the University of Erzerum, and in one form or another Islamic studies are now taught in other universities. Istanbul has an Institute of Islamic Studies within the faculty of letters. Some of the professors are moderately conservative, but academic control appears to be in the hands of liberals. In 1985 the University of Izmir hosted an

International Conference of Qur'ānic Studies in which liberal tendencies predominated.[6] Many of the students attending the courses now provided are going on to become school teachers, so that there is a likelihood that within a decade or two the majority of the younger generation will have a good knowledge of Islam with a liberal slant. Such developments were doubtless easier in Turkey than elsewhere because of the abolition of the Turkish religious institution by Atatürk; but there once again seems to be something like a religious institution, even if in a new form. While Turkish liberals are thus proving very successful in spreading a truer image of Islam throughout the population, they do not appear so far to have produced any outstanding book to attract attention in other countries.

In the Sudan there are some hopes that an adaptation of the Sharīʿa to modern conditions will be achieved. The most powerful political figure there, Ṣādiq al-Mahdī, is known to favour such a course. He wants greater Islamization, but not by trying 'to shape contemporary society in the mould of a bygone intellectual and social past'. He believes that the Sharīʿa is sufficiently flexible to allow this, but in order to bring it about 'the schools of Moslem law must be transcended in favour of a new position bound only by the Quran and Sunnah and capable of dealing with contemporary circumstances.'[7] He himself has written in the Sudanese Mahdist tradition on such matters. As a descendant of the Mahdi and leader of the Anṣār (followers of the Mahdi) he has considerable support in the Sudan, and from his position as premier should be able to accomplish something. There are also strong conservative forces, however, led not by the ulema, who are relatively weak in the Sudan, but by the heads of the sufi orders.

The situation in Indonesia with regard to liberal movements is interesting but very complex. Indonesia claims to be the largest Islamic country with 80 to 85 per cent of its population of 130 millions being 'statistically' Muslims. Within the Muslims, however, a sharp distinction is made between practising Muslims or *santri* and nominal Muslims or *abangan*, so that they are virtually two distinct communities of whom the nominal Muslims are the more numerous. Early in the present century some Indonesian Muslims became aware of the threat to Islamic identity from the political, economic and cultural impact of the West, and as early as 1912 a reformist association was formed called the Muhammadiyya.

Gradually Islam became the focus of resistance to Dutch colonial rule, and this led to a degree of revival of Islam and a recovery of confidence in Muslim identity. This continued under the Japanese occupation from 1942 to 1945.

Since 1945, however, the work of governing and administering Indonesia has been largely in the hands of *abangan* of rather secular outlook, with the result that Islam has become the focus of opposition to Presidents Sukarno and Suharto. In this matter conservative practising Muslims have been more influential than liberals, especially through the organization of Nahdatul Ulama (the Awakening of the Ulema), founded in 1926. The liberals' lack of influence has been largely due to their disunity. Among the liberals Nurcholis Madjid advocated 'the necessity of renewal in Islamic thinking' and founded the Gerakan Pembaharuan or Renewal Movement which flourished in the 1970s, but does not seem to have achieved any positive transformation of the Islamic self-image. In the field of education both the Muhammadiyya and the Nahdatul Ulama have organized schools which combined religious teaching with some 'modern' subjects, while at the higher level State Institutes for Islam have been established which accept pupils from both Western-type schools and the more traditional ones. It is still unclear, however, how far these developments will lead to any appreciable modifications of the traditional world-view and self-image.[8]

In Egypt the university of al-Azhar has been expanded and courses established in 'modern' subjects, but it is not yet clear whether there has been any liberalization of traditional Islamic teaching. There are certainly many Western-educated people in Egypt whose outlook may be described as liberal in a general way, but the ulema are mostly very conservative and have considerable influence, though some are now perhaps becoming more liberal. The Egyptian ulema have the reputation of being subservient to whatever government is in power. Many of the students at the Western-type universities have been attracted to traditionalist movements, possibly because of the difficulty of obtaining employment after graduation; and the same is true of students in Tunisia, which is a comparable progressive country.

A full description of what has happened in Pakistan since independence is given by Fazlur Rahman in his book *Islam and Modernity* (pp. 110–25). It is a sad story of an increasingly repressive conservatism which has made it difficult for liberal intellectuals to express their views openly, although they are an important section of the population. In this respect the Muslims of non-Islamic India are in a much better position. The University of Aligarh, already mentioned, continues to flourish, as does the Jāmiʿa Millīya Islāmīya (or National Islamic University) founded in 1920. A recently formed association of scholars calling itself Bait al-Hikma was able in 1984 to organise an International Conference on the Reconstruction of Islamic Thought.

The best way to appreciate the position of Islamic liberalism at the present time is to look at the work of two outstanding thinkers of today, the Pakistani Fazlur Rahman and the Algerian Mohammed Arkoun. It is significant that neither now lives in an Islamic country, the former being a professor in the University of Chicago and the latter at the Sorbonne in Paris. Both are completely abreast of Western thinking, both historically and in its recent developments. Fazlur Rahman argues convincingly against Hans Georg Gadamer, while Mohammed Arkoun is so steeped in the latest theories current in Paris that it is sometimes difficult for English-speaking readers to follow him. Both are aware of the urgency of working out a new self-image for Islam, while at the same time realizing that this must be done on a genuinely Islamic basis which ordinary Muslims can recognize as Islamic. In discussing educational reform Fazlur Rahman writes:

> Yet the crucial question to which we must eventually seek an answer here is whether there is an awareness among Muslims – and if so how much and how adequate – that an Islamic world-view needs to be worked out today and that this is an immediate imperative. (*Islam and Modernity*, p. 86)

In his book *Islam and Modernity: Transformation of an Intellectual Tradition* Fazlur Rahman was primarily concerned with the creation of an educational system which will be both genuinely Islamic and also appropriate to the world of today. In his programme for achieving this he assigned a central place to a new exegesis of the Qur'ān. Such an exegesis must regard the teaching of the Qur'ān as a whole, and not take particular verses in isolation. It must be based on a study of the historical situation in which a specific rule was formulated, and then move from this to a statement of 'general moral-social objectives' to be derived from it. It is these general objectives which will give guidance in dealing with present-day problems.

Mohammed Arkoun also looks to a new exegesis of the Qur'ān, but speaks in terms of the latest ideas in semiotics and semiology.[9] At the same time he hopes for a recovery of 'the exhaustive tradition' of Islamic thought, by which he appears to mean looking at the various sects not merely as having diverged from orthodoxy, but as having made positive contributions to the development of Islam. Fazlur Rahman hints at a similar attitude when he speaks of the conflict between the Muʿtazilites and the Ashʿarites. What both thinkers seem to be aiming at is a fresh evaluation of the reasons for dismissing as heretical such views as those of the Muʿtazilites.

These two thinkers are perhaps best described as analysts of the present situation in Islam. They have a clear realization of the character of the new world-view or identity which is urgently needed, and they have suggested methods of working it out in detail. They do not regard it as their function, however, to provide the new identity, and it has not been possible for them to become leaders of movements. For such functions a different type of thinker is required, someone who will fulfil the traditional role of a 'renewer' (*mujaddid*). Such a person would probably have to have poetic gifts and be able to stir the imaginations of ordinary Muslims, as well as having the ability to lead people. It may be that several persons will be needed, and it seems certain that the desired end will not be reached without much conflict and suffering.

If we now go back to Sir Hamilton Gibb's assessment of the achievements of Islamic modernism up to 1945, we see that the weaknesses he indicated have largely been remedied by the latest generation of liberal Muslim thinkers represented by Fazlur Rahman and Mohammed Arkoun. They have fully accepted Western historical criticism and are prepared to apply it in the interpretation of the Qur'ān and in a review of the history of Islamic thought. They have also understood that it is essential not to neglect 'the broad and deep currents of a people's psychology' and so have given a prominent place to a fresh study of the Qur'ān. Even if a truer Islamic self-image has not yet been reached, yet considerable progress has been made along the road towards it. After expression has been given to the new self-image, of course, there is still a long way to travel before it is widely accepted. Nevertheless the right man at the right time with the right form of words might quickly gain a very extensive following among the religiously-minded Muslims of Western outlook. This would be particularly likely to happen if some failure of their programmes discredited the traditionalists, whose voices alone are being heard at the moment.

Chapter Five

THE SELF-IMAGE AND CONTEMPORARY PROBLEMS

It is obvious to informed observers that the traditional Islamic self-image is making it difficult for Muslims to adjust adequately to life at the end of the twentieth century. It is also making it difficult for Islamic countries to play the part in world affairs that their populations and strength justifies. Before looking at the problems in detail, however, it will be helpful to look generally at the unsatisfactory features of the traditional world-view and self-image.

1 THE RECOVERY OF A TRUER SELF-IMAGE

Many Muslim statesmen, and others who have to take important decisions, are aware of the special difficulties Muslims have to face nowadays, and may realize that to some extent these are due to features of the traditional self-image. Thus because Muslims have tended to think of social conditions as unchanging, many suppose that a return to the exact form of Islamic social life in the early period would solve all contemporary problems. This supposition is based on a false assumption, however, that of the unchangingness of the world in which we live, especially its social structures. As noted in chapter I, it may be allowed that basic human nature does not change, since some twentieth-century people have proved to be just as wicked as any in the past. What is clear, however, is that Western science, technology and industry have so changed some of the material circumstances in which people live that changes of social structure have inevitably followed.

This is most evident in respect of communications, both actual travelling and the dissemination of information. These two factors make it possible for an individual or a small group to control much vaster organizations than have been known in the past. Large states are more effectively controlled from above than ever before; and enormous economic empires can also be built up. The instantaneous transmission of news means that an incident in one part of the world may provoke public demonstrations in another continent a few hours later. Even more spectacular changes may result from the present computer revolution. Such changes also have negative results. Many of the old skills and crafts are no longer required, and those who practise them sink in the social scale unless they acquire some of the new skills.

For a proportion – sometimes large – of the population of many countries material goods are easily obtainable, and the outlook of such people tends to be dominated by consumerism. At the same time there are increasing disparities of wealth within countries. All this means that many Muslims today are living in conditions which are very different from those of seventh-century Mecca or ninth-century Baghdad, so that merely to imitate what was done in these cities is unlikely to solve today's problems in Cairo, Baghdad, Lahore, Tehran or Jakarta.

The ideal of self-sufficiency also hinders Muslims in dealing with contemporary problems. Many Western-educated Muslims today are only too conscious of the weakening of their religious beliefs by the anti-religious elements in Western thought; but few Muslim religious leaders are aware of the extent to which the anti-religious forces have been opposed by Christian thinkers, and of the possibility of adapting these Christian responses to the needs of Muslims. The unwillingness of the ulema to learn from the West in this repect means that they are unable to help other Muslims with religious doubts, and indeed have no inkling of the depth and complexity of the problems with which such people are dealing. The situation is comparable to that which faced al-Ghazālī in the eleventh century when the ulema were largely unaware of the serious challenge to their teaching from the Falāsifa; but today's challenge is more extensive, since it is not only from philosophy but also from historical and literary criticism.

Perhaps the most acute difficulties created by the traditional self-image are in the area of international relations. Muslim statesmen have, of course, entered into commitments in the United Nations and other international bodies, but there is no precedent for this in the Islamic past. Many Muslims still tend to think in terms of the contrast between the sphere of Islam and the sphere of war. The Egyptian reformist Sayyid Quṭb applied the concept even within his own country, as will be shown later. The Iranian treatment of the American hostages in 1980 and 1981, and then of a British diplomat in May 1987, was not thought to be contrary to the Sharīʿa. In traditional Islamic thinking there was no such entity as diplomatic immunity. The statesmen doubtless observed something of the sort in their relations with foreign powers, but on a pragmatic basis and not because of any formulations by the ulema. In the modern world diplomatic immunity is seen by traditionalists as something imposed by Western colonialism, which need not be taken too seriously. It is certainly no sin from a traditional Islamic point of view to disregard this 'foreign' idea. The traditionalists fail to realize that, if Islamic countries are to be accepted as members of the international community of nations, they must observe the accepted rules. These rules are presumably in accordance with the Sharīʿa, despite the fact that in medieval times they were never formulated.

These drawbacks and difficulties arising from the attempts to live in today's world according to the traditional self-image lead to the question whether this is a sound self-image or whether it has not been perverted in some ways. The conception of unchangingness is not prominent in statements of the Islamic world-view but it is an underlying assumption. Even a relatively Westernized Muslim like Seyyed Hossein Nasr can write: 'For Islam, the crushing evidence is of permanence, that which comprises Islam's central reality. . . . The idea of permanence in Islam permeates the whole Islamic consciousness about itself.'[1] Sufficient has perhaps been said here, however, to show that in important respects changes have occurred in social structures, and that the assumption of unchangingness is false.

The belief in the finality and superiority of Islam is always asserted in a general way and is not defended in detail. The external observer cannot, of course, object to the Muslim holding that his religion is superior to all others, since this is to be expected of the adherents of every religion; but the bare assertion of superiority carries little conviction. One would expect some demonstration of how Islam is superior to other religions in its ability to deal with the problems of the end of the twentieth century. Moreover, the assertion of Islam's superiority to Judaism and Christianity is partly based on the doctrine of the 'corruption' (*taḥrīf*) of their scriptures, which is alleged to be taught in the Qur'ān, but which cannot in fact be justified from the Qur'ān and which is historically untenable.

The belief in Islamic self-sufficiency is patently false. No man is an island, nor is any religion. Islam first appeared in seventh-century Mecca where there were various rival religious beliefs: Arabian polytheism; belief in Allāh as a 'high god' superior to other deities; and some slight knowledge of Judaism and Christianity. The presence of these religious ideas in Mecca does not mean that the new religion was wholly dependent on them or merely a new amalgam of elements from them. I hold that the new religion was a fresh initiative on the part of God; but the forms in which its teaching was expressed (the Qur'ān) owed much to the existing religious situation in Mecca and Medina, if only by way of pointing a contrast; and people's understanding of the Qur'ān had to start from their existing beliefs. Similarly there was a pre-Islamic morality which was accepted and followed in much of Arabia, and this morality was practised also by the earliest Muslims except in respect of those matters where it was felt to be unsatisfactory and where new rules were propounded in the Qur'ān (as in the case of marriage). The belief in Islamic self-sufficiency was supported by the belief in the Qur'ān as the word of God received by Muḥammad with complete passivity – a belief which fails to allow for the human element in the formulation, acceptance and interpretation of the text (as will be explained more fully in the next section). The denial of any human element in the Qur'ān implies that it owes everything to God alone and nothing to the web of human relationships within which Muḥammad and the early Muslims existed.

For the period up to 1600 there is some truth in the view of world-history according to which the Dār al-Islām is advancing and will eventually comprise the whole world, while in the dwindling Dār al-Ḥarb there need only be temporary arrangements. It is perhaps by a kind of extension of this view that some Muslims see the Western world as engaged in a conspiracy to destroy Islam. The traditional division of the world into two spheres is not appropriate to the last four centuries, and fails to give the Islamic *umma* an adequate positive image of its place in the contemporary world.

Again, the idealized image of Muḥammad and early Islam is seen by the external observer as containing many elements which are unhistorical. Why should it be denied that Muḥammad in his youth shared in the polytheistic beliefs of his fellow-Meccans? There are reports which state this, and some verses of the Qur'ān may reasonably be interpreted in a similar sense, notable the word 'erring' (*ḍāll*) in 93.7. Many Muslim writers, too, paint very black pictures of the conditions of life in Arabia prior to Islam, although the plentiful information about the Arabs of the Jāhiliyya shows that such a picture is far too black. It is also virtually certain that conditions under the first four 'rightly guided' caliphs were by no means so idyllic as is often assumed by traditionalists. There was much violence and caliphs were assassinated; and it is also likely that many decisions of public policy were based on Arab custom and not on Islamic principles. As noted in chapter I the punishment of stoning for adultery was probably not practised until some time after Muḥammad's death; and other Islamic laws may not have been finally formulated until the Umayyad period (661–750) or later.

The last few paragraphs show various ways in which the traditional self-image is perpetuating a conception of Islam which in certain respects is false and inadequate. The nature of truth in this matter is by no means simple and obvious. In a discussion of 'Religion as a Cultural System' Clifford Geertz has written:

> In religious belief and practice a group's ethos is rendered intellectually reasonable by being shown to represent a way of life ideally adapted to the actual state of affairs the world-view describes, while the world-view is rendered emotionally convincing by being presented as an image of an actual state of affairs peculiarly well arranged to accommodate such a way of life.[2]

In accordance with this way of thinking it might be suggested that the traditional Islamic world-view, despite the points just criticized, was well suited to be the basis of life for the community of Muslims from the time it received something like its present shape until about 1600. It gave Muslims a feeling of confidence about their place in the world, and it supported the internal balance of power between the religious and political institutions. Thus the world-view, in addition to its other functions, served the interests of those with power of one sort or another by justifying their power. The points just mentioned as being unhistorical probably did not matter in medieval times, since they had no adverse effects on the values presented in the self-image. Thus the traditional self-image, when first given shape, was well suited for its purposes. It is only because conditions in the world have changed that it now requires to be transformed.

In speaking of the need for a transformation of the traditional Islamic self-image I am not attacking Islam as such but am rather trying to help Muslims to make a better adjustment of their community to its place in the contemporary world. To emphasize this point I shall quote a Christian writer speaking about the need for such a transformation in Christianity. The transformation has already occurred to some extent, but it is also continuing into the future:

> There may be a coherence between the teaching and the practice of the Church, but if its basic assumptions are false, then there will be a disharmony between the teaching of the Church and our everyday life, and the teaching presented will split off and become a part of our consciousness which has nothing to do with the rest of our human experience. A Church isolated from our human experience can only survive as long as it can succeed in forbidding its adherents to ask questions and think for themselves. It must lay heavy emphasis on the importance of obedience to religious authority, obedience being understood as unquestioning acceptance of whatever is presented by the teaching authority, and making it sinful for its members to criticise, or to read or listen to anyone who may propose any contrary teaching. . . .
>
> The Church must encourage the critical element in its members. If it fails to do so, then the individual will not be able to integrate religious belief with everyday experience or, put in other words, God will be excluded from most of the individual's life until religion comes to be considered a private but harmless eccentricity of a minority.
>
> If the Church does encourage the critical element, then it must expect to be questioned and challenged by its members and it must be prepared to change its own ways of thinking and acting, submitting itself to the light of truth. Such an attitude is only possible in a Church which has a strong faith in God's presence in all things.[3]

The writer of these words was thinking only about Christianity and his own Catholic religious institution, and not at all about Islam;

but what he says about forbidding people to ask questions and emphasizing 'obedience to religious authority' could almost be a description of the attempts of the Islamic religious institution to stifle discussion of possible changes in the traditional self-image. When the adherents of a religion begin to ask questions – as Muslims are doing today – their questions must be answered at the level at which they are asked, and not treated as acts of apostasy and rebellion. Any other course sooner or later leads to disaster.

2 INTELLECTUAL RECONSTRUCTION

The first point to be looked at is the need for the reconstruction of the intellectual basis of an Islamic world-view. Muslim ulema, by shutting themselves off for centuries from the intellectual life of the West, knew nothing about important new developments taking place there, and were unprepared for dealing with them when contacts increased. Similarly unprepared were the diplomats and students who were sent to the West in the nineteenth century and plunged into the maelstrom of Western intellectual life. In the West there was no one coherent philosophical system but several rival systems. In many of them were incorporated the values of the Enlightenment, and these values were also widely accepted by people, especially the belief in rationality. Most educated people also believed in the soundness of the empirical methods used in the sciences, and came to accept the results on which the main body of scientists was agreed. There was indeed some hesitation in the latter part of the century before it was generally accepted that the human race was descended from lower species of animals, just as there was in the present century about the theories of Freud and Jung.

In some ways the severest shock to the traditional Islamic self-image came from the almost universal acceptance in the West of the results of historical criticism (with which may be included literary criticism). When Western scholars applied their normal historico-critical methods to certain aspects of Islamic history, they reached conclusions which were very disquieting to traditionally minded Muslims. There was no special illwill on the part of most of the scholars. This was simply the point at which the weaknesses of the traditional Islamic self-image were thrown into relief by the encounter with Western thought. The criticism made of orientalists by some contemporary Muslims are thus unjustified. The orientalists were applying to Islam the same ideas and methods which other scholars were applying to Christianity and to secular history. At first many Christians thought that Christianity was being attacked, but gradually Christian scholars learned how to use the same methods to defend Christianity; and even if changes were accepted in secondary points of the Christian world-view and self-image, the final result was a deeper understanding of Christian truth. In the case of Islam one or two scholars, such as David S. Margoliouth and Henri Lammens, were somewhat hostile, but many other scholars were working to correct the distorted image of Islam inherited from medieval times. In my own book *Islam and Christianity Today* I was among other things trying to show how belief in God and in prophethood may be defended in terms of modern thought.

By the late twentieth century most ulema were aware of the extent of the problems caused by the exposure of the Islamic world to Western thought, but had no idea of the depth of these problems. This may be illustrated by the following quotation. It is from the publisher's announcement of a series of books containing (in English translation) revised versions of papers given at the First World Conference of Muslim Education held in Mecca in spring 1977:

> Muslims in the twentieth century are passing through a period of self-examination and self-awareness. The Muslim majority countries that extend from Morocco to Indonesia have adopted the Western system of education in order to acquire modern knowledge so that they may become intellectually and materially advanced. This system of education has long ago been separated from the sphere of the Divine, and is at present secular in approach, since basic assumptions behind Natural, Applied, and Social Sciences and Humanities are not drawn from religion. Along with these concepts, a modern way of life which contradicts the traditional way of life governed by the Sharia is becoming established in Muslim society and is being encouraged by radio, television and other mass media programmes. A cultural duality has therefore appeared in the Muslim world. The traditional Islamic education that still persists is supporting the traditional Islamic group, whereas modern secular education is creating secularists who know or

care little about their traditions and values or pay only lip-service to them.

As the secular education is dominant in Muslim countries, Muslim thinkers have become worried that gradually the Muslim world will lose its identity by losing its Islamic character and will thus suffer from the same moral disintegration and confusion as the West. It can preserve that identity and preserve the Ummah from the confusion and erosion of values and from the conflict between religious and secular groups only if Muslims receive a truly Islamic education. And education can be truly Islamic if Muslim scholars can produce Islamic concepts for all branches of knowledge and Muslim countries can disseminate them among Muslim intellectuals and students. This requires research projects, production of text-books, and properly devised teacher-training programmes.

If Muslim scholars can evolve this system, formulate basic concepts from the religious point of view, and have text-books written on the basis of these concepts, even Western religious thinkers and educationists will find a new dimension to their thinking and thus they will be able to strengthen their efforts to stem the tide that has almost swept away religious values from their system and society.

The quotation shows that among the conservative ulema who dominated the conference there was an awareness of the gulf between themselves and those Muslims with a mainly Western type of higher education. They seemed to think, however, that all that was required was to 'produce Islamic concepts for all branches of knowledge' and to disseminate these. This presumably referred to the 'Western' subjects; there was no suggestion that any of the Islamic so-called 'sciences' required to be modified. A more recent writer has spoken of dealing with the problem as a matter of urgency by 'the development of a science which takes its root from the epistemology and value system of Islam.'[4] By speaking of the value system he seems to mean that the pursuit of science should be subordinated to human welfare – a sentiment with which many Westerners would agree; but by epistemology he can only refer to the epistemological and philosophical basis of the theological aspects of the traditional Islamic world-view, and this is precisely what requires to be reexamined. The remainder of this section is devoted to a discussion of the problems in this area.

(a) The linguistic expression of religious truth

Traditionally minded Muslims seem to assume the complete competence of the human mind to know God and the complete adequacy of human language to express this knowledge. Both these assumptions are dubious, indeed false. In both Islam and Christianity there has been a strain of thought which held that God in his full being is ultimately unknowable by the human mind. There was some discussion of the problem by Muslim theologians in connection with the application of anthropomorphic terms to God in the Qur'ān. Simple-minded persons took these literally, some theologians said they were to be taken metaphorically, and yet others said they were to be accepted 'amodally' or 'without (specifying) how' (*bi-lā kayf*), namely whether literally or metaphorically. The problem needs to be looked at freshly, however, in a modern context.

The most basic words in any language are words for material objects (tree, house), for qualities of objects (blue, heavy), for simple actions (walk, carry) and for simple relationships (on, from). This may be said to constitute the primary use of language, and this enables those who speak it to communicate with one another about the affairs of daily life. When they want to speak about some object for which there is so far no specific word, a word may be used in a secondary sense. Thus the new invention by which electricity is used to give light is called a 'bulb' because it resembles the botanical object so named. It may be called 'electric bulb' where there is danger of confusion, but usually people know from experience how to deal with such bulbs and do not plant them in the garden.

The secondary use of language is very common when people are talking about complex ideas or 'patterns', such as the Iranian 'revolution', the 'expansion' of the Islamic state, the 'impact' of the West on the Islamic world. Much of this secondary use of language is not obvious to us in English as such because we use words derived from Latin and Greek. An 'atom' is simply an 'uncut' entity. This example shows that even in science there is a secondary use of language. Still more instructive is the scientifice use of 'waves' and 'particles' in discussing the nature of light. To the non-scientist this appears to mean that some features of light, as known mathematically, resemble ocean waves while others resemble small material bodies.

In the sphere of religion people are mostly using language in this secondary way. When God 'hears' prayers this does not mean that he has an organ which picks up sound waves, but that somehow or other he becomes aware of the desires of the human suppliant, where, of course, even 'becoming aware' is a secondary usage. What is to be insisted on here is that such terms are not descriptive in the strict sense but only evocative, that is, suggesting or hinting at something whose precise nature is beyond our comprehension. On the other hand, despite the fact that these terms are only evocative, they enable us to engage in the various activities which go to make our religion and which are believed to be important for the life of the human race. Above all they enable us to enter into a meaningful relation with the power on which life is dependent. In practising our religion, then, we have to accept these terms at their face value or 'without asking how'. Simple-minded people do this naturally, but for those who are aware of the complexities of the linguistic question the terms are to be accepted, I suggest, with sophisticated naivety.

In my book *Islam and Christianity Today* I mostly used the term 'symbolic' to describe this secondary use of language, but I have now decided that this word has too many other shades of meaning and prefer 'iconic' instead.[5] An icon is a two-dimensional representation of a three-dimensional reality (a person), and is thus something known to be inadequate, and yet accepted as sufficiently representing the object. A word will be said to be used in an iconic sense when it is known that it only suggests or evokes an object and does not describe it adequately. An important corollary is that, in respect of the iconic use of language, what appears to be contradictory is not necessarily so; the application to God of the term 'transcendent' does not necessarily exclude the term 'immanent'; and, for Christians, the term 'father' does not necessarily exclude the term 'mother'.

The use of the word 'iconic' may also be extended to accounts of historical events in the sacred scriptures which critical historians reject as accounts of objective facts. Examples are the visit of the Wise Men to Bethlehem in the Bible and the presence of Abraham and Ishmael at Mecca in the Qur'ān.[6] The story of the Wise Men or Magi is a way of saying that the birth of Jesus was important for Gentiles as well as Jews; and the connection of Abraham with Mecca evokes what is a genuine fact, namely, the connection of Islam with the Abrahamic tradition. Such accounts, even if not objectively true, may be said to have iconic truth, and are to be accepted 'without asking how' or with sophisticated naivety. The same holds of the details of scriptural events which have to be rejected on scientific grounds, such as Noah's flood and the crossing of the Red Sea by the Israelites during their exodus, while the Egyptians drowned.[7]

(b) The human element in revelation

The next point to consider is the traditional Islamic conception of the Qur'ān as the word of God; 'speech of God' would be a more accurate rendering of *kalām Allāh*, but 'word of God' is preferable because of its English connotations. What has to be criticized is not the belief that the Qur'ān comes from God, but the further belief that the eternal is somehow present in language without the admixture of anything human. A little reflection shows the impossibility of this. The problem was appreciated by some Muslim scholars, and they spoke of the Qur'ān as being not the word of God itself, but only an *ʿibāra* or *dalāla* or *ḥikāya* or *rasm* of the word of God, and by these terms they seemed to mean something like an 'indication' or 'representation' of it.[8]

In so far as the Qur'ān is in the Arabic language, this is in itself a human element. A language does not just happen to exist, but has been made by a human community in a forgotten past. A language is also closely linked with the way in which the community speaking it sees the world, and that includes the basic categories of its thinking. The Arabic language, too, far from being the language of the angels as sometimes supposed, reflects the social customs of Arab nomadism, such as *ijāra* or the giving of neighbourly protection. When this word is used iconically in the assertion that 'God protects but protection is not given against him' this requires much explanation to make it comprehensible to those not familiar with life in seventh-century Arabia.[9] Thus the Qur'ānic word of God does not give us the eternal in its purity, but an evocation or icon of the eternal linked with human affairs. It should really be obvious that human beings can only begin to comprehend the divine through the evocative or iconic use of human language. This is one way in which there is necessarily a human element in revelation. Something human is also present in the process of understanding the divine message, because in this the recipient cannot be purely passive since he has to interpret the words in the light of his general outlook and his own past experience.

A further point is that the Qur'ān contains what Western historical criticism can only regard as palpable errors. A relatively unimportant one is that Mary the mother of Jesus is apparently confused with Miriam the sister of Aaron (19.28); both would be Maryam in Arabic. More important is the apparent denial that Jesus was crucified and died on the cross (4.157), and the assertion that Christians worship three gods (4.171; 5.73, 116). The death of Jesus through crucifixion is one of the most certain facts of all ancient history; and it is also known that since two and a half centuries before Muḥammad the great majority of Christians have been repeating weekly and sometimes daily a creed beginning with the words 'I believe in one God'. There seem to have been obscure Christian sects which could have been accused of believing in three gods, but it is doubtful if they comprised as much as one per cent of Christians. Once it has been admitted that there are errors of fact in the Qur'ān, how is it to be accepted as the word of God in the traditional Islamic understanding of this phrase? I have suggested in various places[10] that a Muslim could take the view that God had adapted the wording of the Qur'ān to the outlook of the people of Mecca, among whom these erroneous opinions were current, and that it was not part of the purpose of the revealed message to correct such errors. This suggestion, however, is unlikely to receive much attention from liberal Muslims.

What would be much more credible to the modern Western outlook would be to hold that the messages came to Muḥammad from his unconscious (in a Jungian sense). This would be in accordance with his experience of the messages coming to him from beyond himself, since the unconscious is beyond the self in the sense of being beyond the conscious mind. Moreover the unconscious is still a somewhat fluid conception which has not yet received a definite place in a Western philosophical system; and this certainly leaves open the possibility that God may work through a prophet's unconscious. The unconscious is closely associated with consciousness in that what comes into a person's mind from his unconscious is expressed in terms of his conscious world-view, though the unconscious would appear to have also an inner forward-looking dynamism from which novel thoughts may come. Something like this is part of what Christians understand by the Holy Spirit, who 'spoke by the prophets' according to the Nicene creed. If the Qur'ānic messages can be regarded as coming into Muhammad's conscious mind from his unconscious in some such way, then that will explain both how they are expressed in terms of the current Meccan and Arab world-view, including its errors, and also how they represent a divine initiative.

This account of the prophetic experience is one which could also be applied to the Old Testament prophets. Each spoke to the people of his time in ways that these could understand. The prophets themselves, too, were usually aware that they belonged to a succession of prophets, and that each was continuing and developing the messages brought by his predecessors. At the same time, however, there was in the prophecies of each something new which they held to come from God; in other words there was a divine initiative, and the phrase 'Thus says the Lord' was used. In suggesting, then, that the Qur'ān came to Muḥammad from his unconscious I am not denying its divine origin, but placing it on the level of the Old Testament prophecies. All that is being denied is one simplistic way of understanding what it means by saying that the Qur'ān is the word of God.

Christians nowadays regard the Old Testament prophets as each having been sent by God with a message for a particular human situation, and not simply with statements of general principles. Thus Jeremiah was sent with a series of messages for his contemporaries, who were first fearfully expecting, and then actually experiencing, the destruction of the kingdom of Judah. In the case of Muḥammad the human situation for which he received a message from God was the social and religious malaise in Mecca as a result of its commercial prosperity.[11] In so far, however, as the factors in a particular situation are factors which are found in other situations, then the message for the particular situation will have a much wider relevance, possibly universal. Jesus once said that he was sent only to the lost sheep of the house of Israel, but nevertheless his message was universal. The spread of Islam shows that the message given to Muḥammad had a similar universal relevance.

(c) The uniqueness of Islam

In its origins the conception of Islam as self-sufficient probably owed something to the Muslim Arab community's feeling that it was superior to the weak 'tribes' of Jews and Christians under its protection. More recent expressions of self-sufficiency have been influenced by the view that the Qur'ān is the word of God, pure and uncontaminated by anything human, since God is assumed to act with complete autonomy. The last few paragraphs should have shown conclusively that such a conception of Islamic self-sufficiency is untenable, but this must not be taken to imply that Islam is no more than a pale copy of other religions. Despite some dependence on Judaism and Christianity, there is much in Islam that is unique and distinctive, and this aspect of the matter must now be looked at.

All religions grow out of a pre-existing religious situation by introducing some new elements which modify what is already present. In Mecca it is known that there were relics of the earlier Arabian polytheism. The Qur'ān itself, however, provides evidence that many people in Mecca and the surrounding region believed in Allāh as a 'high god' while continuing to acknowledge other deities; and this may well have been the dominant view among Muḥammad's contemporaries.[12] At the same time the intellectual outlook of Mecca was permeated by certain Jewish and Christian ideas, though the knowledge of these religions was very incomplete and was mistaken in some points.

Out of this strange amalgam of ideas in pre-Islamic Mecca what may properly be regarded as a divine initiative selected certain themes which were specially relevant to the religious and social situation there, and at the same time introduced new themes. In the earliest passages of the Qur'ān the main themes were: God's goodness and power; God as judge on the Last Day; his demand from his servants of gratitude, worship, generosity with their wealth, and the like; and his sending of Muḥammad as a prophet.[13] These themes were relevant in Mecca because of the arrogant pride and unscrupulous conduct of the wealthy merchants who dominated the life of the community, while at the same time there had been a breakdown of the traditional nomadic morality and of most forms of religion. In themselves these themes, apart from the prophethood of Muḥammad, belong to the Judaeo-Christian tradition, but the selection of points to be asserted and the relative emphasis given to them is something unique to Islam. Thus Islam is not simply a continuation of Judaism and Christianity, but a distinctive religion, separate from them but parallel. The best way to express this is to say that Judaism, Christianity and Islam are three branches of the religion of Abraham. (This conception will be expanded in section 6.)

(d) The acceptance of historico-critical methods

The aspect of Western thought which has been found most disturbing by Muslims is probably the general acceptance in the West of the results of historical criticism, with which may be included the literary criticism which applies similar methods to the study of texts. When orientalists, as noted above, seemed to be attacking Islam, they were usually doing no more than apply to Islamic materials the methods used by Western scholars in all branches of history. Although the aim of historical criticism is primarily to discover what are the objective facts, a work of history is not merely a collection of objective facts, but requires that some facts be selected from a large accumulation of facts in order to present a picture in which certain values are high-lighted; and it is in this way that there may be a place in a work of history for material which is iconic and not objective fact.

Some of the instances of the overturning of traditional Islamic conceptions by historical criticism have already been mentioned, such as the errors of fact found in the Qur'ān. Much of what was described in chapter I as the idealization of Muḥammad and early Islamic society is also of very dubious truth. Muḥammad must have shared in the un-Islamic beliefs of his fellow Meccans when he was a young man. Muslims did not become perfect when they accepted Islam either in respect of their memories or in other ways. Thus the variant readings of the text of the Qur'ān are to be seen as due to mistakes made by the transmitters. And early Muslim society was by no means a society without problems.

It should not be necessary for Muslims to idealize Muḥammad and the early Muslims in an unhistorical way. He and they have many great achievements to their credit which are matters of objective fact. What Muslims have to learn here is that God works even through human imperfections, and can bring about great things despite human errors and mistakes. When the Bible tells how David committed adultery and then put the woman's husband in a position where he would be killed,[14] the modern historian cannot reject the fact; but the believer realizes that despite the weakness in David shown by this serious lapse God was able to make use of his outstanding qualities, and that David was nevertheless a very great man.

(e) The acceptance of Western science

The importance of science and science-based technology and industry in the modern world is beyond question; and the acceptance of science is an essential part of the Western outlook. Within this acceptance, however, a distinction has to be made. It would be agreed by most intelligent people that one must accept the assured results of science, that is, what the general body of scientists accepts, and must also accept the general validity of scientific methods as ways of discovering truth about the world. On the other hand, there are various assumptions of a philosophical character associated with science which the believer in God is bound to reject; for example, that the only realities are those presently being studied by science. This body of assumptions may be referred to as scientism or physicalism. A critique of scientism was given in my *Islam and Christianity Today*, and so need not be repeated here.

Among the assured results of science that have to be accepted is descent of the human species from lower forms of life. At a superficial level this contradicts both the account of creation at the beginning of the Bible and the scattered references in the Qur'ān. What has to be realized is that it is not the purpose of the sacred scriptures to present a scientific cosmology. Their concern is to show how the human race and its environment is related to God, and they do this with complete adequacy provided they are understood as making iconic statements.

Another point at which there is apparent discrepancy between scriptural assertions and the results of science is in the miraculous events in which God allegedly interferes with the laws of nature in order to punish, reward or save human beings. It is an axiom of the scientific outlook that scientific laws, if properly established, cannot be broken. From this it follows that, if a miracle is an event in which the laws of nature are interfered with, then it is an impossibility. This does not mean, however, that the believer must simply reject all the accounts of miraculous happenings in Bible and Qur'ān. In some cases, such as miracles of healing, it is possible that the accounts are true, and that we have evidence of the working of forces not yet adequately studied or understood by scientists. In other instances, such as Noah's flood, it would appear that the account of some real happening has been distorted in the course of transmission; and here the story is to be taken iconically and accepted with sophisticated naivety, so that we may appreciate the lessons it is teaching us. This last attitude is also appropriate where no real happening seems to underlie the story, such as the alleged miracle of the clay birds made by Jesus which then came alive.[15]

These would appear to be the chief points at which a basic intellectual reconstruction of the Islamic world-view is necessary, if it is to get rid of the false and erroneous elements and achieve a truer image of the place of Islam in the contemporary world.

(a) It must realize that the truth about God cannot be fully comprehended by human minds and cannot be fully expressed in human language; statements about divine matters can be no more than evocative and iconic.
(b) A human element is present in the messages from God contained in the scriptures.
(c) Islam is not independent of other religious and intellectual movements either in its origins or in later times, but it nevertheless has a unique place, along with other religions, in God's purposes for the world.
(d) The methods of historical and literary criticism must be accepted, and lead in the end to deeper understanding, even if some inessential and secondary points of traditional belief have to be abandoned.
(e) Something similar is true in respect of the acceptance of the results and methods of science.

3 THE LINKING OF RELIGION AND POLITICS

Traditionalist Muslims normally hold that Islam cannot be truly and fully itself except in an Islamic state, that is, a state ruled by Muslims and where the Sharīʿa is the law. Some go even further and say that there should be only a single Islamic state for all Muslims not under alien rule. This conception is bound up with that of the Dār al-Islām or sphere of Islam, which will be considered more fully in the next section. This linking of Islam with politics is also seen as a necessary form of opposition to Western attempts to privatize Islam and make it a purely personal matter.

(a) The changing shape of the Islamic polity

From the time of the Hijra the Muslims constituted not merely a religious community but also a body politic. This is an important difference between early Islam and early Christianity, since for three centuries the latter was not a political entity. Many Muslims, and not only traditionalists, regard the state and community formed by Muḥammad as something distinctively Islamic, and at one time I took a similar view and spoke of the Islamic state as a 'theocratic polity'.[16] The document commonly called the Constitution of Medina,[17] however, which appears to have been the basis of political life there after the Hijra, shows that the polity was not something novel, but was essentially a confederation of tribes or kin-groups in accordance with traditional Arab principles.[18] This confederation became Islamic not through some special Qur'ānic rule, but by the fact that the main contracting parties were all Muslims. Muḥammad was spoken of as 'prophet' and had the right and duty of settling disputes, but otherwise no special political privileges. There is, of course, nothing surprising about this. A new political structure cannot be created out of the blue any more than can a new religion. This structure of a federation of tribes persisted until the end of the Umayyad period and beyond. Non-Arabs becoming Muslims had first to become clients (*mawālī*) of one of the members of the federation, that is, an Arab tribe; and the stipends paid by the government to fighting men and others were paid through the tribes.

When Muḥammad died and Abū-Bakr became his 'caliph' (*khalīfa*) or successor, this was in part a new development, but the office of caliph seems to have been essentially that of the chief or *sayyid* of a tribe or federation, except that this federation was much larger than any hitherto known in Arabia. There seems to have been a somewhat informal council of leading men whom the caliph could consult. As the federation expanded into an empire the power of the caliph increased greatly. In the empire were many non-Muslim groups or 'protected minorities' (*ahl adh-dhimma, dhimmīs*), who were not full members of the polity; they were dependent groups under the protection of the federation, not federated tribes. With the transfer of power from the Umayyad to the 'Abbāsid dynasty in 750 ideas derived from the traditions of Persian statecraft were incorporated, and the rule of the caliph became more autocratic.

After less than two centuries, however, the shape of the polity changed once again. By 945 the ʿAbbāsid caliphs in Baghdad had lost practically all their political power. The Islamic empire was divided among a number of sultans or war-lords who ruled various provinces through the power they had from command of an army. Almost all these war-lords, however, found it expedient to have a form of legitimation, namely, to have a nominal appointment from the caliph as governor of those territories which they had in fact seized by military might. This ʿAbbāsid caliphate without political power came to an end in 1258 when the Mongols captured Baghdad. After that date there was a caliphate of sorts in Egypt, not recognized outside Egypt, and from this caliphate the Ottoman sultans claimed to have inherited the title of caliph. By this time, however, it was little more than an honorific title, and it was abolished by the Turkish Republic in 1924. A pan-Islamic conference on the caliphate in 1926 failed to reach any agreement about the restoration of the office of caliph.

These matters are mentioned here to throw into relief the fact that Islamic history offers no clear model for a truly Islamic state today. In the past Muslim statesmen have been pragmatists, using whatever political ideals seemed helpful in their particular situation; and in the present century something similar seems to be happening. In some Islamic countries there have been attempts to establish democratic forms, and this receives a measure of justification from the verse 'their affairs are [by] counsel between them' (42.38); but this is a relatively recent development. During the last forty years, after the attainment of independence and the establishment of some democratic forms, these have frequently been replaced by dictatorships, after either a 'movement of national liberation' or a *coup d'état*.[19] Autocratic rule based on military power is very much in the Islamic tradition, and in today's world it can get further support from its control of information; but it can hardly be claimed that this is the ideal Islamic state.

(b) The legitimation of rule

The question of the legitimation of rule in an Islamic state can be approached by a quotation from Mawdudi:

> An Islamic state must in all respects be founded on the law laid down by God through His Prophet. The government which runs such a state will be entitled to obedience in its capacity as a political agency set up to enforce the laws of God and only in so far as it acts in that capacity.[20]

The idea that the legitimacy of a ruling institution is dependent on its upholding the Sharīʿa can be traced far back in Islamic history, but not to the very beginnings. The first four caliphs came to the office in various ways.[21] The form of accession, which may be called nomination in one case and election in the others, was followed by an acclamation or oath of allegiance (*bayʿa*). It seems to have been with the ʿAbbāsid dynasty that the upholding of the Sharīʿa became an element of legitimation. By 750, when the ʿAbbāsids came to power, there was a religious institution at least in embryo, and this had for the most part supported them against the Umayyads. In return it was recognized in some sense by the caliphal government; and this meant that its formulations of the Sharīʿa would be applied by the law courts. This was the beginning of a kind of alliance between the ruling institution and the religious institution. The latter proclaimed the legitimacy of the ruler, and in return was acknowledged as having authority to formulate the Sharīʿa as well as to administer justice. When the ʿAbbāsid caliphs lost all political power and were replaced by war-lords, the religious institution produced arguments for the legitimacy of these last in addition to the fact that they were nominally appointed as governors by the caliph.

In a sense, then, it may be allowed that from 750 onwards Mawdudi is roughly correct in saying that rule gained legitimacy from its upholding of the Sharīʿa; but in practice this meant that the rulers acknowledged the rights of the religious institution. In this symbiosis of the political and religious institutions, however, there is an element of collusion. The Sharīʿa as formulated by the ulema covered various aspects of law – civil, criminal, personal, commercial – but the ulema did not try to insist that all governmental decisions should be based on the Sharīʿa. Some theorists did in fact formulate rules for the conduct of war, but there was no attempt to get these carried out by the army commanders. There were many spheres in which a ruler was allowed to act autocratically according to his own ideas without regard for Qur'ānic or other Islamic principles.

When one looks at contemporary Islamic states, it is clear that the form of rule adopted has depended less on Islamic precedents than on the pragmatism or improvisation of those who wield power. Mostly the ulema have received only a modicum of recognition. In question of personal status the Sharīʿa or something like it may be in force, but in other respects the laws owe more to Western legal thinking. Reforming conservatives have criticized the ulema for their subservience to governments. On the other hand, when governments have felt weak, they have tried to pacify conservatives by the reintroduction of the Islamic penalties of amputation for theft and stoning for adultery, though, even where these were made legal, they seem to have been carried out only to a limited extent. In other words, this may have been mainly a gesture. In many minor respects the statesmen have tried to show that they were good Muslims. Their states join or support various international Islamic bodies; and they themselves publicly join in prayers. In all this, however, they may be said to be merely using Islam. Their deepest motivations are not Islamic, and they fall far short of Mawdudi's ideal of upholding the paramountcy of the Sharīʿa.

(c) The relation of religion to politics

Traditionalist Muslims claim that in Islam religion and politics are inseparable, and that Western attempts to privatize Islam are an attack on it. The question which both Western observers and Muslims have to face is whether this is a true assertion or whether it is no more than an argument (of dubious validity) in order to buttress the status of the ulema in Islamic society. One can ask, for example, whether it is possible to be a Muslim in a non-Islamic state; and the answer must surely be in the affirmative. It is true, of course, that in its origins Islam was both a religious community and a body politic, and it is natural that this should remain an ideal condition for Muslims. It does not follow, however, that one cannot be a Muslim except in an Islamic state. Through the centuries Muslims have been traders and in the course of their work have travelled into non-Muslim countries and even settled there; but they have not ceased to be Muslims.

If one looks dispassionately at the position of a Muslim in a non-Islamic state, such as the established Western states, there is little to hinder him from practising his religion. He will not be forced to drink alcohol or eat pork. He will be protected by a criminal law similar to the Sharīʿa, though its penalties may seem to him to be less severe. There may be difficulties if a Muslim man wants to have more than one wife, but these difficulties would probably be chiefly about claims on a welfare state in addition to those for a first wife and family. For some Muslims the most serious difficulty will be having to send teenage daughters to schools with mixed classes. Yet this is precisely one of the points at which the traditionalist interpretation of the Sharīʿa is being questioned by many Muslims. Apart from this, however, there is the consideration that, if Muslims want to live in a Western country, they should be prepared to share in its customs and not make themselves into a kind of ghetto. Education of a teenage girl, or indeed boy, in a mixed school should be a good preparation for life in a society in which there is a large measure of freedom for men and women to mix.

Very relevant to this assertion that Islam demands statehood is the creation of the state of Pakistan. It seems probable that the idea of having a separate Islamic state was mainly fostered by the perception that in a united India Muslims would be unfairly treated by the Hindu majority; and this may well have been a true perception. It does imply, however, that Pakistan was created in order to defend the material interests of Muslims. Originally conservatives like Mawdudi opposed the idea of a separate Islamic state; and this is not surprising since the arguments for Pakistan used by Mohammed Ali Jinnah were largely secular.[22] In the end, however, it may have been the old idea of Dār al-Islām that won over the Muslim masses. Nevertheless the creation of Pakistan meant that some forty million Muslims were left as a less significant minority in a more predominantly Hindu India. Those Muslims who advocated the policy of remaining in a united India, such as Mawlana

Azad, may have had a deeper understanding of the true nature of Islam.

In practice the demand for statehood seems to be no more than a demand that the state should observe such provisions of the Sharīʿa as are commonly (or perhaps ideally?) formulated by the ulema. As already noted, this does not cover all the decisions of the ruling institution. Even where the Sharīʿa was being applied, it was admitted – in the Ottoman empire, for example – that there were areas of detail where the administrators had to use their judgment. It is difficult to resist the conclusion that the assertion of the inseparability of religion and politics in Islam is primarily an assertion of the political importance of the religious institution. A Muslim writer who appears to accept something like this view of the matter further argues that the fact that in Islam religion has not been privatized is due to the absence of a strong and self-confident middle class, capable of opposing the exaggerated claims of the ulema.[23]

It should not be assumed, however, that there is no middle way between the upholding of the Sharīʿa by the state and a complete privatization of religion. The life of the citizens of a modern state is now highly complex and elaborately organized, and legislation has also to be complex. There would seem to be room for a distinction between the general moral and ethical principles implicit in the Sharīʿa and the detailed application of these principles in legal enactments. If such a distinction is recognized, it will follow that the expertise required for formulating the principles is different from that required for framing the legislation. It might then be possible to have a division of labour, with the formulation of principles being assigned to the ulema, and the framing of laws being the work of statesmen helped by civil servants. The problem has been recognized by some conservative Muslims, and one suggestion is that there should be ulema specializing in a particular field of legislation, such as car insurance or embryo research. Whether such a system would be feasible would depend on the general political structure. Where there were democratic forms, there would also have to be provision for the views of ordinary people to be represented. Any such ideal division of labour, however, seems to be far removed from the political structures of actual Islamic states, except perhaps Iran. There is also the question whether in this sphere everything can be left to the expert, or whether ordinary people may not have a moral outlook which is worthy of respect.

Some Muslim writers take the view that there is little concern for morality in Western politics. Mawdudi goes so far as to say, in speaking of the system of representative democracy:

> a divorce has been effected between politics and religion and, as a result of this secularization, the society and particularly its politically active elements have ceased to attach much or any importance to morality and ethics.[24]

It may be true that in the West in the political discussion of many current issues self-interest seems to be dominant, but fundamentally the bulk of legislation is based on the moral principles inherited by Christians from the Old Testament and to a lesser extent from the ideals of the Roman empire. The welfare of the poor and unfortunate is also an important concern of modern Western states. For some centuries the West has tended to assume that there was a moral outlook shared by all citizens, and that this was essentially the Christian moral outlook. Latterly, however, the study of moral principles has been divorced from theology and entrusted to a separate class of moral philosophers; and in the present century the moral philosophers have ceased to be interested in the normative aspects of the subject and in the giving of guidance in moral dilemmas. Thus to an external observer like Mawdudi it may seem that not much importance is attached to morality in politics.

Things are beginning to change in the West, however. By the time of the First World War there were many Christian pacifists who held that participation in war is sinful; and the number of pacifists has been greatly increased by the invention of the nuclear bomb. There is now, too, greater attention to medical ethics because of the need for legislation about abortion and similar matters. Church leaders are also speaking out on other contemporary political problems, and being reprimanded by the politicians for interfering in what is not their business. The politicians probably think that they themselves are sufficiently expert in moral questions, and may also differ from the Church leaders on points of detail. It seems likely that in the next decade much more attention will be given to the development of a normative ethics on a Christian basis, and one from which the political application will not be excluded. If this happens, it will open up the possibility of useful discussions between Christian moralists and the suggested Muslim experts in the formulation of general moral principles, since these principles are nearly the same for both, despite differences in detail in such matters as marriage. The application of moral principles to the legislation and administrative practice of a state is a continuing process, since new problems keep arising, and since injustice or unfairness may come to light in fresh quarters or may develop in the course of time. It is to such discussions that Muslim experts would probably have a contribution to make.

The conclusion to be derived from all this is that there is no justification for the assertion that Islam cannot be Islam except in an Islamic state under a Muslim ruler who upholds the Sharīʿa. In most Western states at the present time a Muslim can be a good Muslim and practise all the main duties of his religion. Underlying the assertion, however, is an important truth with which Christians would agree, namely, that any state will be imperfect unless it is based on moral values such as are implicit in the Sharīʿa and also on belief in God as upholder of morality and justice. This is also true of an international organization like the United Nations.

4 INTERNATIONAL POLITICS

The field of international politics is one where the traditional self-image is making it particularly difficult for Muslims to play a part commensurate with their strength and their ideals.

(a) The perception of a hostile world

Islamic history provides no models which might guide Islamic countries as they seek an appropriate place within an international community. In pre-Islamic Arabia the major tribes were independent political units, and so in a sense constituted a multiple community, though each normally only had relations with its close neighbours. In some respects there was a common mode of conduct based on a common culture. There could also be alliances and federations from time to time. The most obvious 'international' feature here was the law of retaliation. If a member of one tribe was injured or killed by a member of another tribe, the former tribe would attempt to exact vengeance from the latter; and vengeance was usually exacted even if the original victim had been in some sense to blame for what happened. It is difficult not to see this pattern being followed in some of the events of 1987. A minor

Iranian diplomat in Britain (without full diplomatic privileges) was accused of a petty offence and of further offences in trying to avoid arrest. Apparently in retaliation for this a senior British diplomat in Iran (with full diplomatic privileges) was kidnapped and beaten up, and only released after high-level protests. Something similar happened between Iran and France, except that the original accusations were more serious.

By the time of Muḥammad's death the Islamic state was already stronger than any of the Arab tribes, and its strength went on increasing, so that the model of the Arabian tribal community became irrelevant. After the state had grown into an empire the only comparable body with which it was in contact was the Byzantine empire, though there were minor powers in Western Europe and on the eastern frontiers. With some of these the caliphs had diplomatic relations at least occasionally, and presumably there were some diplomatic conventions which were observed most of the time. This was a matter, however, which was in the hands of the Muslim statesman and not to be interfered with by the ulema. Thus the religious institution never reached the point of working out Sharīʿa-based rules for the conduct and treatment of emissaries between different states. Had they done so, they would probably have reached results not unlike the international 'diplomatic immunities' of today. As things are, however, these have no place in the traditional Islamic world-view, and are seen as a Western invention which is being imposed on Muslims in the interest of the West.

According to the traditional self-image the place of Islam in the world is defined by the distinction between Dār al-Islām and Dār al-Ḥarb, as was explained in Chapter I. This is a kind of extrapolation of the remarkable expansion of the Islamic state in the century after Muḥammad's death. The Dār al-Islām, where the Sharīʿa is fully observed, is seen as continuing to expand – perhaps inevitably – until it includes the whole world. Meanwhile the non-Islamic part of the world is seen as potentially hostile, as the Dār al-Ḥarb or sphere of war. It was realized after a time that the Islamic frontiers had sometimes receded, but the withdrawals were regarded as temporary; and until about 1600 there was some justification for this last idea.

Muslim traditionalists today also hold that the expansion of the Islamic state was not colonialism, but was the bringing of a fuller spiritual life to people hitherto deprived of it. Orientalists who imply that the Islamic expansion was colonialist are charged with making false accusations, although they were in fact trying to defend Islam from the charge of being a religion which spread by the sword (part of the medieval 'distorted image' in European eyes); they tried to show that the expeditions which brought about the Islamic conquests were essentially expeditions in quest of booty, in line with the Arabian nomadic tradition of the *razzia*. This is fairly obvious if the sources are read objectively. Moreover in the western half of the Islamic empire most of the conquered peoples did not at once become Muslims but had the status of 'protected minorities' (*ahl adh-dhimma*). In Arabia itself in the earliest period pagans and polytheists were probably given a choice between Islam and the sword, but elsewhere Jews, Christians, Zoroastrians and even Hindus were regarded as 'peoples of the book' and became protected minorities. The Hindus were accepted as monotheists because of their philosophers, despite the obvious polytheism of ordinary people.

The perception of the world as hostile to Islam goes back to before the Hijra. Many of the earliest passages of the Qur'ān are critical of the attitudes and practices of the Meccan merchants, and the latter naturally took up a hostile position towards Muḥammad and his followers. After the Hijra and the attacks by Muslims on Meccan caravans, the hostility received a military expression. Thus the last ten years of Muḥammad's life can be characterized as a military struggle against opponents, not in order to bring about the spread of Islam, but in order to ensure the survival of the Muslims.

This perception of hostility has received a new dimension during the present century as a result of Muslims' study of history in the West. Many Muslims now see colonialism as a continuation of the aggression of Christians against the Islamic world begun by the Crusades. This is in no way a folk-memory but is a new perception based on what Muslims have learnt in the West, perhaps begun by Muḥammad ʿAbduh. Doubtless there is some justification for their seeing the Crusades as an early stage of the struggle between the Islamic world and Christian Europe for the southern and eastern shores of the Mediterranean.

The attitude to the use of force in religion is an important point of divergence between Muslims and Christians. Traditionalist Muslims, and many others as well, hold that the right of a Muslim to observe the practices of his religion should be defended by force of arms if necessary. In a recent book one finds the sentence: 'When the right of a Muslim to practise his faith is denied by any power, he must either fight back in self-defence, and become a *mujāhid*, or if he cannot fight or fails in this fight, he should emigrate and become a *muhājir*.'[25] (*Mujāhid* is the active participle corresponding to *jihād* as *muhājir* to *hijra*.) This is, of course, a somewhat crude attempt to apply the ideas of Muḥammad's time to modern conditions. Many Christians appear to hold that it is not necessary to defend Christianity in such a way, and it was a result of this attitude at least in part that they acquiesced in the steps which led to the state of Israel. There was also an important body of Christian opinion, however, which objected to the handing over of the Christian holy places to the Jews. The central point here seems to be that, while a religion is primarily something spiritual, yet its physical embodiment is also important, and indeed is a part of it; and Christians should probably be doing more thinking about this.

The place of the Jihād or 'holy war' in Islamic thought must also be looked at. The word properly means 'striving' or 'effort', but there are several instances in the Qur'ān of the phrase 'those who have striven in the way of God with wealth and person',[26] and this is taken to mean participating in expeditions where there was a possibility of fighting. There are also verses permitting or commanding fighting. The earliest is probably: 'permission is given to those who fight because wronged' (22.39). Another early verse is: 'fight them [the Meccan unbelievers] until there is no persecution and the religion is God's alone' (8.39). A verse which may formulate the policy guiding the later conquests is: 'O you who have believed, fight those near you of the unbelievers, and let them feel harshness from you' (9.23).

The concerns of seventh-century Muslims illustrated by these words are echoed in a passage by Mawdudi, first written in 1932, and quoted here from the revised English translation of 1960. After speaking of the need to be ready to make sacrifices to protect the interests of Muslims and of Islam, he went on:

> *Jihād* is a part of this overall defence of Islam. *Jihād* means struggle to the utmost of one's capacity. A man who exerts himself physically or mentally or spends his wealth in the way of *Allah* is indeed engaged in *Jihād*. But in the language of *Sharīʿah* this word is used particularly for the war that is waged

> solely in the name of Allah and against those who perpetrate oppression as enemies of Islam. This extreme sacrifice of lives devolves on all Muslims. If, however, a section of Muslims offer themselves for participating in *Jihād*, the whole community is absolved of her responsibility. But if none comes forward, everybody is guilty. This concession vanishes for the citizens of an Islamic State when it is attacked by a non-Muslim power. In that case everybody must come forward for *Jihād*. If the country attacked has not the strength to fight back then it is the religious duty of the neighbouring Muslim countries to help her; if even they fail, then the Muslims of the whole world must fight the common enemy. In all these cases, *Jihād* is as much a primary duty of the Muslims concerned as the daily prayers or fasting are.[27]

This statement by Mawdudi is entirely in line with the teaching of the ulema throughout the centuries, which has been summarized as follows: 'In law, according to general doctrine and in historical tradition, the *djihād* consists of military action with the object of the expansion of Islam and, if need be, of its defence.'[28] Some of Mawdudi's phrases might suggest the pipe-dream of an academic, and one wonders whether he really expected his rulings to be carried out with twentieth-century weaponry. Yet events in the Iraq-Iran war show that there are Muslims who believe it a duty to act in such ways. Ayatollah Khomeini, who regards his Iraqi aggressors as apostates and unbelievers, has said:

> Defending an Islamic country and Muslims' honor is a divine obligation. Due to observing Islam, we always oppose war and would like peace to exist among all countries. But if a war is imposed on us, the nation will confront it powerfully, if it is even supported by all superpowers.[29]

How deep is this sense of living in a hostile world may be illustrated by V. S. Naipaul's description of an old *maulana* or teacher in a theological school in a small village in Pakistan in late 1979:

> he was alive with a religious passion that was like malevolence: the passion for the true faith running, as it can easily run, into the idea of Islam in danger, the need for the holy war, the idea of the enemy.[30]

Closely associated with the idea of the holy war is an element in recent Muslim thinking sometimes called Mahdism. Strictly speaking, Mahdism among Sunnites means belief in the appearance of a divinely inspired leader, the 'guided one' or Mahdi, who will by force of arms set things right in the world. Whereas Shīʿites believe that their Twelfth Imam is still alive and will at an appropriate time return as the Mahdi, for Sunnites the identity of the Mahdi is not known until he appears. Sir Hamilton Gibb, speaking in 1945, saw the essence of contemporary Mahdism not in the emphasis on a leader but in the conviction that 'the Muslim world must be purified and reunited by the sword'.[31] He further saw this as an emotional reaction to the impact of the West on Islamic society, and a revolt against a state of affairs felt to be intolerable, but a reaction without any clear and detailed idea of what was to be set up instead, apart from a commitment to the restoration of the Sharīʿa. Gibb foresaw the likelihood of more violent Mahdist reactions as a danger threatening Islam, since 'the heresy of Mahdism is its belief not only that the minds and wills of men can be dominated by force but that truth can be demonstrated by the edge of the sword.'[32]

Since 1945 there have been a number of instances of such reactions, not least the occupation of the Great Mosque in Mecca in 1979 by a handful of zealots. Groups among the Muslim Brotherhood in Egypt, too, were attracted by Mahdism, not with any positive aims, but in order to give vent to their feelings of frustration and despair at the existing state of affairs. Very illuminating is a passage from the report of the trial of Sayyid Quṭb in 1966 when he was accused of being involved in terrorist plots, condemned and executed. The term *jāhilī* had been used by him in this passage to distinguish between *an-niẓām al-islāmi*, a truly Islamic social order, and *an-niẓām al-jāhilī*, one in which Muslims had become decadent and had reverted to the outlook of the Jāhiliyya (the condition of Arabia before Muḥammad). Describing the views of Sayyid Quṭb the prosecutor said:

> The leaders of your *tanzim* (apparatus) said that you led them to understand that they are a community of believers (*umma mu'mina*) in a *jāhilī* society, and that nothing binds them to the state or society or current government, and that as an Islamic *umma* they must consider themselves in a state of war with the

> state and with the society in which they live; that you designated the rest of the country as a *dar al-harb*, and thus any acts of murder or destruction are not crimes but pious acts for which there is religious sanction.[33]

Sayyid Quṭb was clearly not far from the desire for martyrdom which has become almost normal among the followers of Ayatollah Khomeini.

(b) Islam in the world of nations

There is justification in past history for Islam's perception of hostility to itself in the rest of the world. There is even a measure of justification for the Iranian perception of America as 'the great Satan'. This is more than an expression of the dualism which has been prominent in Iran since the time of Zoroaster. It is unfortunately true that one of the great evils of the present day is the unscrupulous exploitation of the Third World by Western multinational corporations, and that America has a leading role in such operations, although all Western countries are involved in them and benefit from them. The Ayatollah Khomeini may use greatly exaggerated language, but some of his assertions should be taken very seriously:

> America is the number one enemy of the deprived and 'mustaz'af' (oppressed) people of the world, and it does not refrain from any crime to extend its political, economic, cultural and military influence over the dominated world.
>
> We, who say that we intend to export our Revolution to all Islamic countries, and even to all countries where the 'mostakberin' (arrogant) rule over the 'mustaz'afin' (deprived), want to create a condition that no oppressive, cruel or murderous government can exist any more.[34]

Some Westerners are aware of the shameful ways in which Western economic power is treating the Third World; and this is offset only to a slight degree by the charitable activities of some Western individuals and non-governmental bodies. It is important, however, that those able to influence the policies of the Western nations should be more fully aware of the depth of feeling underlying this criticism of the West, especially since there are signs that the

Ayatollah is having some success in getting this view of America and the West widely accepted in the Third World.

This perception of Islam as confronting and struggling against a largely hostile world, though it still has some justification, is completely mistaken in important respects.

Firstly, there is what is best called the world economic system. Though the West is by far the largest partner in it, it also includes to some extent the Soviet bloc, China and the Third World. The Islamic countries are part of this system, and not all are mere junior associates without any say in what happens. Some Islamic countries, including Iran, because of their oil wealth, have a considerable stake in the world economic system and considerable influence in it, especially when they act jointly as in OPEC. It has to be remembered, too, that the world economic system, though at several points it has to be severely criticized, is on the whole beneficial, since it is this system which makes it possible for much of the world's population to enjoy a reasonable standard of living. Closely bound up with the economic system is the Western cultural system. In general Islamic countries as a whole and many Muslim individuals want to share in the benefits of Western science-based technology and industry. Even Ayatollah Khomeini chose to return to Iran in 1979 in a jet plane, though he could have made the journey in some other – more Islamic? – way. There are many Muslims who travel to the West as visitors and others who come to study. There are even not a few Muslims who want to share in the intellectual outlook of the West in everything except religion. In the light of such factors it is a mistake to see Islam as standing embattled against a hostile world. It is an important part of the one world.

Secondly, it should be emphasized that some of the elements in the West which are perceived as attacking Islam intellectually are doing so not out of hostility to Islam particularly but out of hostility to religion in general. Sufficient has been said on earlier pages about the similar attacks on Christianity and the Christian response to these. With regard to apparent attacks on Islam which are primarily economic or political, it will be found that in most cases the central motive is not hostility to Islam but the pursuit of selfish interests by individuals and groups.

Thirdly, it should be realized that, despite the innate selfishness of human beings, there is among many individuals and groups in the world a readiness to co-operate for the promotion of human welfare generally. Moreover this co-operation is based on the common acceptance of moral and social values, and these values are to a great extent also accepted by Muslims. In other words there are many people in the world alongside whom Muslims could work for the fuller realization of common human values, including what the Ayatollah describes as the absence of oppression.

These considerations point to the need for Muslims to abandon the image of themselves as confronting a world hostile in all respects. Instead of seeing the non-Islamic world as Dār al-Ḥarb they should see it as a sphere in which there are opportunities for them to co-operate with non-Muslims in good works of many kinds. As a basis for such co-operation, however, Muslims would require to make certain admissions.

The most important requirement is to admit that religious and moral systems other than Islam, even if they are far from perfect in Muslim eyes, may contain a large measure of truth. Muslims would, of course, continue to hold that Islam is religiously and morally superior, but they would also have to recognize that the adherent of any moral and religious system normally thinks that his system is superior to others. Since there is no generally accepted criterion to distinguish between the truth and falsehood of such systems, co-operation between the adherents of different systems requires that all should admit that the others are true at least up to a point, and it is usually unnecessary to specify in what respects each is true. In other words, Muslims are required to accept a pluralism of religions and moralities, and to see themselves as one community within a pluralistic world. A corollary would be that they might possibly have something to learn from some of the other systems.

It is in the application of moral values to social and political life that co-operation would appear to present fewest problems, at least intellectually. The relation of morality to religion is a difficult question because, though we may speak of Christian ethics and Buddhist ethics, morality is to a great extent independent of religion, and is based rather on the nature of human beings. At the same time, however, religion helps individuals to live more in accordance with their moral beliefs. The life of all human communities is based, among other values, on those implicit in the fifth to the ninth of the Ten Commandments in Exodus 20, which may be stated positively as respect for parents, for life, for marriage and for property, and truthfulness in public statements. Recognition of these values is also assumed as part of the basis of the United Nations and other global institutions, though there is still much to do before all international political activity is based on moral principles. Since these values are all upheld by the Sharīʿa, Muslims should have no difficulty in co-operating with others who are working for a fuller incorporation of moral values into the life of human beings at all levels.

Muslims might also be expected to admit that the nature of warfare and fighting in the late twentieth century is very different from that in the seventh century. This would mean that some of the Qurʾānic commands to fight cannot be applied in contemporary conditions. A state would still be entitled to defend itself when attacked, but it is difficult to imagine any circumstances in which modern warfare could be used for the spread of religious belief. Muslims should also remember that there was an element of realism in the traditional understanding of the Sharīʿa in this matter. 'The duty of the *djihād* is relative and contingent . . . it only comes into being when the circumstances are favourable and of such a nature as to offer some hope of a victorious outcome.'[35] This places strict limits on regarding modern warfare as a permissible form of *jihād*. Muslims in general seem to have given little attention to the moral questions raised by the development of military technology. A few, however, have considered the question of nuclear weapons and have argued that their use is contrary to the Sharīʿa.

5 SOCIAL ISSUES

Islamic countries today are faced with many new social problems. Most of these are the inevitable result of the technological and industrial developments of the last two centuries, which have been made possible much larger conurbations, much larger political units and more rapid communications. Because Islamic societies want to have the products of industrial technology, they cannot avoid the problems.

(a) Opening the gate of Ijtihād

In the nineteenth century some Muslim intellectuals and statesmen realized the problems that were emerging, and began to speak of the need for 'opening the gate (or door) of Ijtihād'. This was a way of describing the adaptation of the Sharīʿa to modern conditions. Ijtihād is primarily the expenditure of effort. In legal matters it is contrasted with *taqlīd* or the following of precedents, and so implies the determination of a legal rule by going back to first principles; the translation 'independent judgment' is sometimes used. A more precise definition is:

> the effort to understand the meaning of a relevant text or precedent in the past, containing a rule, and to alter that rule by extending or restricting or otherwise modifying it in such a manner that a new situation can be subsumed under it by a new solution.[36]

The four recognized Sunnite legal schools or rites came into existence about the ninth century as a result of the exercise of Ijtihād by their founders. There is no record of any formal statement that the gate of Ijtihād had been closed, but it came to be held by the great majority of ulema that the exercise of Ijtihād was no longer permissible. In actuality, too, no new legal schools came into existence after about the year 900. Some Ḥanbalites did not accept the prohibition, and went on exercising Ijtihād, though without saying so. It was almost certainly one of the later nineteenth-century Muslim reformers who first spoke about the need to reopen the gate of Ijtihād, and not the orientalists, as some recent conservative Muslim apologists have claimed. In chapter 5 of *The Spirit of Islam* Ameer Ali complains about the prohibition of Ijtihād in respect of the rules for marriage.

In the later nineteenth century and afterwards, even when the ulema agreed on the need for reform of the law, they were unwilling to do so by the exercise of Ijtihād. A number of changes were in fact made, but by way of what might be called expedients. Thus in Egypt child marriage was not explicitly forbidden – which would have been difficult since Muḥammad married 'Ā'isha when she was nine – but the courts were forbidden to deal with matrimonial cases in which at the time of marriage the husband had been under 18 and the bride under 16. Similarly the modern scientific view of the length of pregnancies was not accepted by the ulema, since in Islamic history there were alleged cases of pregnancies of two, four or even five years; instead the courts were directed not to consider claims for alimony where a pregnancy of longer than a year was alleged.[37] These rulings were based on the traditional right of rulers to determine the competency of courts. Another expedient was to find a suitable legal rule in the work of some early scholar, even though he belonged to a school other than the official one of the country and perhaps to a minority in that school.

Even after it has been admitted that the gate of Ijtihād must be reopened, it is by no means clear how reformers should be proceeding. Fazlur Rahman writes:

> It is also something of an irony to pit the so-called Muslim fundamentalists against the Muslim modernists, since, so far as their acclaimed procedure goes, the Muslim modernists say exactly the same thing as the so-called Muslim fundamentalists say: that Muslims must go back to the original and definitive sources of Islam and perform ijtihād on that basis.[38]

In particular Fazlur Rahman wants much deeper study of the principles of jurisprudence and a working-out of Islamic ethics on a Qur'ānic basis, but he considers that in the existing religious institutions law-making has been stagnant for so long that they are incapable of carrying out the fresh tasks which he envisages. Somewhat inconsistently, as it would appear to an outside observer, he thinks something may be achieved at the university of al-Azhar as now reconstituted.[39]

The non-Muslim can only wish Muslims well as they set about the colossal tasks confronting them. As was suggested above, part of the solution of the problems would seem to be in accepting a distinction between the theoretical and the practical aspects of law-making, and this would fit in with what Fazlur Rahman advocates. A study of the principles of jurisprudence and of the Qur'ānic ethical system would belong to the theoretical, and might be assigned to ulema if they were prepared to work at this; but it could also be carried out by liberal intellectuals. The actual framing of laws, on the other hand, could be left to statesmen, parliamentarians and civil servants, who would be presumed to do this in accordance with Islamic values, but would also have some knowledge of the practicalities of law-making and of the spheres to which the laws applied.

(b) Some particular social problems

This is not the place to attempt a comprehensive review of Islamic social, ethical and legal thinking, but consideration may be given to one or two points where weakness is evident.

A matter which has attracted adverse attention in the West is the restoration of the Islamic penalties for theft and adultery. A distinguished Muslim lawyer has written:

> Nearly all the penal provisions contained in the Qur'an reflect the social conditions which were characteristic of the Arabian tribes 14 centuries ago, and to treat them as binding today would in many cases be a lamentable anachronism. An outstanding example is the law of talion. To maintain, in legislating today, that commandments laid down 14 centuries ago are invariable and binding for all time is to defy the primordial law of evolution and to ignore the spirit of the Qur'an which attributes the quality of permanence only to spiritual values. All other aspects of life on earth are necessarily subject to change, and no enlightened community would legislate on a contrary principle.[40]

The amputation of a hand to punish theft is explicitly commanded in the Qur'ān (5.38), and may have been appropriate in seventh-century Arabia, but it is certainly not a suitable punishment in a modern society. As already noted, it may be seen as in part a punishment of the family for the misdeed of one of its members (in accordance with ideas of family solidarity); but today a person incapable of doing normal work is a burden on the whole community. Besides the aim of penal legislation is to bring about a society free from crime, and experience seems to show that severe penalties do little to promote this aim.

In the Islamic resurgence one of the points emphasized as distinctive of true Islam is the prohibition of interest on loans. This is based on Qur'ānic verses in which *ribā* is forbidden (2.275–80; 30.39), but the precise meaning of *ribā* is uncertain and there have been divergent views. Nowadays, however, the traditionalists insist that it means lending of money under whatever circumstances at a fixed rate of interest. It is virtually certain that the Qur'ān did not intend to forbid any financial practice in the realm of commerce current in Muḥammad's time, since the Muslims were a business community. It is likely that the prohibition was made in order to stop a Muslim taking advantage of another Muslim's misfortune. This certainly seems to have been the purpose of the somewhat similar rules in the Old Testament; for example, 'if you lend money to any of my people, to any poor man among you, you must not play the usurer with him; you must not demand interest from him' (Exodus 22.25); but when money is lent to foreigners interest may be taken (Deuteronomy 23.20).

In the economic system proposed today by Muslim theorists from a traditionalist background loans at a fixed interest are to be replaced by loans for production on the basis of profit-sharing. 'Islamic' banks have been established to operate this system, and these are also supposed to be ready to grant interest-free loans for consumption to suitable persons. There is something to be said for the view that those who make production-loans to an industrial company (or, as a Westerner would say, buy shares in it) should take a measure of responsibility for its policies. For consumption-loans, however, it is difficult to see how a bank could decide between the needs of possible recipients. There are poor people, too, who would prefer the security of a fixed rate of interest for their money to the uncertainty of a possibly higher rate of interest from a company. And how can a person who invests £100 in a multi-million company have any effective responsibility for what it does? His best course is to find some other company of which he approves and buy shares in it; and there are Western Christians who believe in selective investment of this kind. A little examination shows that this 'Islamic' economic system has not been sufficiently thought out to make it viable for Muslims, still less as a system for non-Muslims. At too many points it presupposes that the wealthy are all ideal Muslims, wholly altruistic and ready to put their social responsibilities above personal gain.

In a somewhat similar vein there have been attempts to adapt the traditional Islamic concept of *zakāt* (alms-giving) as part of an ideal Islamic economic system. A Muslim whose capital (for example, in camels), or in other cases whose income, was above a certain amount had a duty to give away a percentage of it to the poor and deserving. Unfortunately contemporary writers only agree about the *zakāt* on those forms of wealth which existed in early medieval times, and have not been able to suggest a fair and just application of these norms to the vast fortunes of some Muslims at the present time, when there are many new forms of wealth. The idea underlying *zakāt* is excellent, namely, the duty of the well-to-do to assist those suffering from poverty and other difficulties. In our complex modern societies there may be serious oversights if the care of the poor and unfortunate is left solely to the initiative of individuals, though much has undoubtedly been done in many spheres by wealthy Muslims. Some organization of welfare by the state, however, is nearly always also required. This would appear to be an instance where the moral principles implicit in the Sharīʿa could be formulated by the ulema, namely, the responsibility of the whole community, both the ruling institution and individuals, for the welfare of the poor; and it could then be left to politicians to correlate public and private activity and to work out suitable forms of tax.

In Muslim eyes one of the aspects of the moral decadence of the West is its consumerism; and many Westerners would agree that there is an excessive interest in and reliance on material goods, including new and ultimately useless gadgets. Consumerism, however, is something from which wealthy and even not-so-wealthy Muslims are by no means immune. There are now gross inequalities of wealth not only in Western countries but also in some Islamic countries; and there is also gross financial inequality between the wealthy sector of the world (which includes some Islamic countries) and most countries in the Third World. These are problems which should concern the whole of humanity. The principles underlying *zakāt* could have some application here, but it is for Muslims to work out the detail. It would certainly seem that the wealthy in the world should be required to give away (or to pay in tax) a much higher proportion of their wealth than is envisaged in the traditional rules for *zakāt*.

There is an excellent exposition and critique of recent Muslim views on these topics in an article on 'The Economic System in Contemporary Islamic Thought: Interpretation and Assessment' by Timur Kuran.[41] In his conclusion he traces the many unsatisfactory features of writings about Islamic economics to two methodological flaws. One is the failure to admit fully the contrast between the complex economic issues of the modern world and the economic 'blueprint' provided by Qur'ān and Sunna. The second is the disregard of historical evidence, especially of the fact that the economic norms of the Sharīʿa were formulated only gradually, and that in the process some practices of Muḥammad's own time were modified or abandoned.

(c) Human rights

Human rights have had an important place in public opinion throughout the world since the promulgation of the Universal Declaration of Human Rights in 1948. The United Nations have a commission for human rights charged with monitoring how far they are being observed or infringed in various countries; and there are also voluntary bodies such as Amnesty International which have a similar purpose. Many countries have been accused of minor infringements of human rights, but there are also some which have been charged with major violations, and among these are certain Islamic countries. For this reason Muslims have become somewhat sensitive to the question of human rights, and exaggerated and unhistorical claims have been made. A recent writer maintains that:

> centuries before the appearance of modern democracies, the idea of human rights was clearly present in the Holy Qur'ān and the precepts of the Holy Prophet of Islam (peace be upon him). It was this concept of human rights which was afterwards elaborated by Muslim jurists in the most scientific manner under the two-fold division of the rights of God (*Ḥuqūq Allāh*) and rights of human beings (*Ḥuqūq al-ʿIbād*) which included the rights of non-Muslims living in an Islamic state and society.

Among these rights is 'the right to express one's opinion freely', and, after giving an illustration from the life of the fourth caliph, the writer continues:

> This shows clearly that any person may form any opinion or entertain any idea and he may freely give expression to it and the Islamic state will not do any thing to prevent him from doing so, but if he tries to impose his opinions and ideas on others by violent means so as to create social disorder, action will be taken against him.[42]

The writer may be correct in holding that the right existed and had been formulated; but it was clearly not being observed in the examples given above of the totalitarian attitude of the ulema, and it is clearly not being observed in the treatment of the Ahmadiyya in Pakistan today.

It may be allowed that Islam improved greatly on the Jāhiliyya. In pre-Islamic Arabia the individual had no rights as an individual, but only as a member of a kin-group. If you met someone in the desert and did not like his looks, there was nothing to stop you killing him except fear of the retaliation of his tribe. That is to say, the right to life depended on the 'protection' (ability to exact vengeance) of the kin-group. When the Islamic *umma* replaced the kin-group, this right was clearly founded more securely, as were other rights. The rights of the Universal Declaration, however, are mostly the rights of the individual over against the ruling institution, and in Islam the ruling institutions have usually been strong, and have often had autocratic and dictatorial tendencies. This did not bode well for the observance of the rights of the individual. There have been men, such as Aḥmad ibn-Ḥanbal, who have been ready to stand up for the rights of the ulema against the rulers, but hardly any who were concerned to uphold the rights of ordinary individuals.

During the last twenty years or so there have been a number of writings and declarations by Muslims about human rights. Many of these are described and discussed in a number of the periodical *Islamochristiana* devoted specially to this topic, and texts of various documents are also given.[43] The earliest important statement is the Memorandum of the Saʿudi Ministry of Foreign Affairs, drawn up in response to a letter from the United Nations Commission on Human Rights dated 1970. In this it was insisted that in Saʿudi Arabia human rights were guaranteed by divine revelation. Saʿudi Arabia refused to adhere to the Universal Declaration, and expressed disagreement with three points, namely, the possibility of a Muslim woman marrying a non-Muslim, the possibility of a Muslim abandoning Islam for another religion, and the right to form trade unions and to strike. Shortly after the issue of this memorandum there was a colloquium of Saʿudi and European jurists at Riyadh (March 1972) at which these and some other questions were discussed and the Saʿudi position defended.

A more extensive colloquium took place at Kuwait in December 1980 arranged jointly by the International Commission of Jurists, the Union of Arab Advocates and the University of Kuwait. An account of the proceedings was published in 1982 under the title of *Les droits de l'homme en Islam*, and the Conclusions and Recommendations are produced in *Islamochristiana* (78–91). At certain points this colloquium was critical of actual practice in some Islamic states. It was sufficiently authoritative to ensure that the question of human rights was taken up at the ensuing meeting of heads of Islamic states under the aegis of the Organization of the Islamic Conference, held at Ta'if in January 1981. For this a Draft Declaration of Human Rights in Islam was prepared, but not discussed owing to lack of time. It was apparently a form of this draft declaration which was approved at Dhaka, Bangladesh, in December 1983 and at Casablanca in January 1984 at meetings of the Organization of the Islamic Conference. This declaration is more conservative than the conclusions of the Kuwait Colloquy. In September 1981 a Universal Declaration of Human Rights in Islam was promulgated in the UNESCO building in Paris by the Islamic Council of Europe, which is a voluntary association and not an official body.[44] In this Declaration each right mentioned is supported by a quotation from the Qur'ān or the Ḥadīth. Its general position is similar to that of the Ta'if and Dhaka declaration.

These documents show, as one might have expected, that most of the rights of the Universal Declaration of 1948 are in accordance with the Sharīʿa. The really important question, however, is about the extent to which they have been observed in Islamic countries in the past and the extent to which they are being observed today. The *Times* correspondent reporting (12.12.83) on the approval of the declaration of human rights at Dhaka – to be known as the Dhaka Declaration – could not avoid remarking on the irony of this in view of the number of people in Bangladesh at present under restraint without trial. The Kuwait Colloquium was aware of this problem and recommended (no. 16) the establishment of an Islamic Commission of Human Rights. This indeed is the crux of the matter. How can there come into being in Islam a strong body of opinion seriously concerned with the maintenance of human rights? One would hope that within the ruling institutions there would be genuine concern for human rights; but there would also have to be some independent commission or other organization to monitor the behaviour of ruling institutions if these proved recalcitrant. If such an organization was established, there would be ample opportunities for it to co-operate with non-Islamic bodies with similar aims.

It should also be noted that there is justification for Muslim criticisms of the secular character of the Declaration of 1948. The rights mentioned in it were those which the members of the United Nations at that date were concerned about and able to agree on. There was, however, no clear theoretical basis, so that, if in course of time some modifications are desired, it may be difficult to see how to get agreement about them. Here again is seen the need for a normative theory of ethics or moral philosophy, and this is something to which Muslims should be able to contribute.

(d) The position of women

One of the points which has been emphasized in the Islamic resurgence is that Muslim women should not wear Western clothes in public, but should dress in accordance with Islamic standards in 'legal attire' (*az-ziyy ash-sharʿī*). In Iran this is interpreted as the *chador*; in Egypt it is taken to be clothing which leaves only the face and hands uncovered, but some enthusiasts for the resurgence wear a face-veil and gloves.[45] Besides the question of modesty in dress there is that of the general rights of women. Most conservative spokesmen, while they may claim that in Islam women are equal to men, are unwilling that women should engage in other than domestic duties. The Declaration on Human Rights of the Islamic Council of Europe has no section on the rights of women, only one on the rights of the wife; and these include that of being supported by the husband. Thus in the traditionalist world-view, as commonly understood, women are restricted to domesticity.

The objection to Western forms of female dress and the opposition to the free mixing of men and women in the work-place and elsewhere are perhaps not surprising when one considers the great upheavals in Islamic society brought about by the impact of the West. For those who had never seen unveiled women apart from their own relatives the appearence of a mini-skirt on the streets could be a traumatic, indeed a threatening experience. It is suggested in some quarters that the traditional view of the Muslim male is that woman is more sexually active and that segregation and veiling are necessary for male protection. Even apart from this, however, the move from the traditional forms of Islamic urban social life to those of the mid-twentieth-century West must at first have been very disturbing for both Muslim men and women. There was more to it also than psychological disturbance. An Egyptian writer's view are described as follows:

> Muhammad al-Bahi dreads the consequences of women's economic independence: They would avoid family ties and decide for themselves who or if they will marry, where they will live, and whether they will have children. Al-Bahi assumes that if men are not in charge of women, women will lose sight of all human values and the family will disintegrate.[46]

Some writers have gone so far as to accuse world feminism of being part of an imperialist plot to destroy Islamic society, and this has led them to insist on the centrality of women in preserving the moral character of the nation.[47] It is difficult for the outside observer to avoid concluding that much of the enthusiasm for 'Islamic' dress and the segregation of women is due to the fear of the ulema and other males that they will lose traditional male privileges. There are also Muslim women who fully approve, but this is not necessarily the reason why women wear Islamic dress. Since in many cities women in Western clothes have been molested in the streets, some have adopted Islamic dress as a protection; and some Muslim women may feel that they are not ready for the full openness typical of Western society.

It is worth remarking that in the past there has been much variation in what was regarded as appropriate dress for women. There are millions of Muslim peasant women who worked in the fields and never veiled their faces. In Jerusalem in the 1940s Muslim women wore black cloaks with a black face-veil, while those in neighbouring Hebron had blue coats and over their heads a long blue scarf to keep in place a flowery muslin face-veil which made them look like skeletons. By that time most middle-class women in Cairo had abandoned the veil (following Huda Shaʿrawi in 1922), but some poorer women still had a form of face-covering which left the eyes free. Many Westerners will admit that rapid changes in what is permissible in female clothing are undesirable, and that therefore in Islamic countries some restrictions are appropriate as a temporary measure; but in the long run there will have to be much deeper discussions about how female modesty is to be defined.

The more serious question, however, is whether women are to be confined to domesticity and segregated or whether they may work outside the home and mix up to a point with men. A return to segregation, no matter how much conservatives may argue for it, would now seem to be impossible. In Egypt, Syria, Turkey and other countries there are now many well-educated women in important positions in the universities, in literature, in the world of music and entertainment and other spheres. In Pakistan Benazir Bhutto is a potential candidate for the position of prime minister. In Iran, though restrictions were placed on women's work immediately after the revolution, some of the statesmen are now saying that women's labour will be needed to help to build up the country after the war ends. Unless the conservatives in such countries become much stronger than they are at present, it is unlikely that there will be any extensive retrogressive measures; for one thing, the contribution of women to the functioning of these countries as modern states is now so considerable that there would be great difficulty in replacing them. Other countries, however, are more backward. In Saʿudi Arabia virtually the only sphere outside the home open to women is that of female education; and they are not even allowed to drive cars. Presumably the oil wealth of Saʿudi Arabia makes it relatively easy to keep women in the home, but it is doubtful if the present degree of segregation can be maintained indefinitely. The wealthier Saʿudi women can hardly avoid learning about life in the West from films and television and then wanting to have some share in it, especially if they have also travelled in the West, as many have done, and if they know of the achievements of women in other Islamic countries.

In the West many Christians and others are deeply concerned at the aspects of moral decadence obvious in their society, and are working to reverse the trend towards greater sexual permissiveness. Such people would be prepared to learn from the Islamic world if it could come up with a practical alternative. This might happen if Muslims were prepared to abandon complete segregation – something they seem almost bound to do in so far as they want to be part of the one world. They could formulate Islamic norms which put some curbs and restrictions on the free mixing of men and women; and, if these could be shown to work in practice, there would probably be groups in the West which would be ready to adopt them. It may also be pointed out that the continuation of segregation exposes a wealthy woman to the danger of becoming a victim of consumerism, so that she spends lavishly and unnecessarily on fashionable clothes and the other luxuries she sees advertised in the glossy Western and Westernizing magazines which she reads.

6 ISLAM AND OTHER RELIGIONS

One of the minor points at which the Islamic world-view is badly in need of correction is in its conception of other religions and the relation of Islam to these. Islam is a religion based on revelations from God to a single prophet, and the Qur'ān therefore seems to assume that other religions were also based on what was revealed to a single prophet. In particular Judaism is held to be based on the revelation to Moses, and Christianity on that to Jesus. It was further assumed that the revelations to these two, as well as to all other prophets, were the same as that to Muḥammad, at least in essentials. It was to explain to Muslims how contemporary Judaism and Christianity had come to differ from Islam that later Muslim scholars elaborated the doctrine of the corruption (*taḥrīf*) of the Jewish and Christian scriptures.

No other religions are mentioned as such in the Qur'ān apart from three references to the mysterious group called Sabaeans (Sābi'ūn), in one of which the Magians or Zoroastrians (Mājūs) are also mentioned (2.62; 5.69; 22.17). The existence of other religions is allowed for, however, in such verses as 40.78, which speaks of messengers sent by God before Muḥammad, only some of whose stories have been told him, and 45. 28, where in the course of the Last Judgment unnamed communities are 'called to their Book'. Any such religions, however, were presumably regarded as the result of revelations to a single prophet or messenger, so that there was no place in this conception of religion for any idea of development.

This Qur'ānic idea of religious history is clearly inadequate in respect of both Judaism and Christianity. In Judaism there was a long series of prophets. Judaism goes back at least as far as Abraham, Isaac and Jacob. It was from the God of Abraham that Moses received the call to lead God's people out of slavery in Egypt, and to give them the Torah or law; but Moses had a much fuller understanding of God than had Abraham. Moses was followed by other religious leaders like Joshua, Samuel and David, and then by the series of great prophets, such as Isaiah, Jeremiah and Ezekiel, whose books are preserved in the Old Testament, but who are not mentioned in the Qur'ān. These prophets accepted the teaching handed down to them, but received revelations which went beyond that and gave guidance for the problems of their own day. In particular the Israelites were helped to understand God's reason for sending his chosen people into exile and later restoring a remnant of them to their land. Christianity, too, was still incomplete at the death and resurrection of Jesus. The book of the Acts of the Apostles tells how the first Christians came to a fuller understanding of God's purposes through receiving the gift of the Holy Spirit, and how they set about organizing the Church, though this organization was incomplete until the ecumenical councils of the fourth century.

Again, the assertion of Muslim scholars that the Jewish and Christian scriptures have been corrupted is valueless, since no attempt has been made to prove it in detail. It carries no conviction at all with anyone who is aware of the vast amount of historical material that exists about the two religions. At the same time, however, it is true that all religions are living and organic activities of the human spirit, and that they therefore grow and develop. Moreover the growth and change is not necessarily always for the better. Some Christians today are inclined to think that Christian theology became too Hellenistic in the course of the discussions of the third and fourth centuries, so that certain Semitic elements of the faith were neglected. Many also feel that since the seventeenth century Christianity has become too privatised. Once Christians become aware of these deficiencies, they have the possibility of correcting them through the aid of the Holy Spirit.

The idea that the Jewish and Christian scriptures are corrupt has doubtless contributed to the view, widespread among traditionalist Muslims, that the West is morally corrupt and utterly depraved, and to the complementary view that only in Islam is truth and morality to be found. In Indonesia V. S. Naipaul found a young enthusiast for Islam in whose eyes 'Islam was pure and perfect; the secular dying West was to be rejected';[48] this man was the president of an important youth organization attached to a mosque in a middle-class area. What such beliefs amount to is that in Muslim eyes there is no other real (effective) religion in the world apart from Islam, and no other forces working for the good of the human race. This view is probably strengthened by the fact that most of the Qur'ānic accounts of other prophets describe how God supported them against unbelieving adversaries; such accounts were appropriate at the time when Muḥammad was suffering from bitter opposition.

There are a few passages in the Qur'ān which express some positive appreciation of Christianity. In one verse Christians are compared with Jews and idolators and said to be 'the closest in love to the believers . . . because among them are priests and monks, and because they are not proud' (5.82); and in another (57.27) God is said to have placed kindness and mercy in their hearts. Virtually none of this positive appreciation, however, appears in later Muslim writings about other religions, of which there was a certain amount during the medieval period.[49] Mostly these were seen as diverging at various points from the true revelation which they were supposed to have received about God and the Last Day. There were also pagan religions which were human inventions without any basis in revelation. Such an outlook means that the traditional Islamic world-view does not envisage the existence outside Islam of any movements successfully promoting religious and moral values. There are thus no groups of people from whom Muslims might expect co-operation in the building of a better world.

The assertion that Muḥammad is 'the last of the prophets' is bound up with this view of the world religions, especially when it is also asserted that Islam has abrogated the previous revelations. The assertion is an interpretation of the Qur'ānic phrase 'the seal of the prophets' (*khātam an-nabiyyīn*) found in 33.40. To the first hearers this probably meant that the revelation to Muḥammad was the seal confirming the previous revelations, but it is now almost universally taken to mean that he is the last of prophets, after whom there will be no other. This links up with the conception of an unchanging world in which there is no development. In this respect Islam differs from Christianity. Though Christians believe that the Christian revelation is final in respect of essentials, yet they also believe that there is further truth to be learnt about God and his ways, and that for this they receive guidance from the Holy Spirit (as promised by Jesus in John 16.13). For Muslims the concept of Ijtihād gives the possibility of adapting the Sharī'a to changed conditions, but, doubtless because of the belief in unchangingness, little has been done to frame a general theory for such a use of Ijtihād.

Though the phrase 'chosen people' is not used by Muslims, there is a sense in which they do in fact think of themselves as God's chosen people, who alone have divine truth in its purity for communication to the rest of the human race. Perhaps they should have their attention called to the words of God, spoken through another prophet more than a thousand years before Muḥammad to another group who thought they were God's chosen people: 'you only have I known of all the families of the earth; therefore will I punish you for all your sins' (Amos 3.2). The word 'known' implies known intimately and specially, and so loved and chosen. In so far as Muslims claim to have a full and pure knowledge of divine truth, they must also expect to be questioned by God, for example, about how they have observed or violated the human rights they have formulated on the basis of God's revelation.

It would appear to be a minor aspect of the resurgence that many Muslims have come to use Allah in English for the Being they worship. This is presumably a way of saying that there are corrupt features about the Jewish and Christian conceptions of God, and that only in Islam is the true conception to be found. This usage, however, is based on muddled thinking. *Allāh* is no more than the Arabic equivalent of the English 'God', and as such is not exclusive to Muslims, but is also used by Arabic-speaking Jews and Christians. In Mecca, too, about the year 600 there were even pagans who believed in *Allāh* as a 'high god' superior to the other gods they worshipped. A better way of stating the claim implicit in this recent usage would be to say that the Islamic conception of God is entirely true, whereas the Jewish and Christian conceptions are false in various ways. At the same time it is important to recognize that human worship is directed towards not a conception or a name but a Being, and that people holding different and perhaps imperfect conceptions of this Being may yet all be genuinely worshipping him.

Strangely enough, it is in Iran under Ayatollah Khomeini that there is a more obvious positive appreciation of movements with similar aims to the Islamic revolution. On 12 January 1979, shortly before his return to Iran, the Ayatollah published an advertisement in the *New York Times* addressed to the 'Christians of the world'. Much of his message consisted of blessings and greetings, including greetings to the clergy and to freedom-loving Christians. There were also warnings to leaders of Christian countries not to support the Shah.[50] Some of this message appears to have been reproduced along with further material in the propagandist monthly *Imam* published in English in London. One passage runs:

> The Christian clergy have many peculiarities, as the superpowers are Christian or lay claim to Christianity. In contradiction to the words of Almighty God, the superpowers act against Jesus Christ's teachings. According to the teachings of Christ and the Almighty God, the Christian clergy have a duty to wage a spiritual war against the superpowers who act contrary to the way of the prophets and the way of Christ.[51]

Iranian interest in gaining Christian support is further shown by the holding in Tehran in March 1985 of a seminar of Muslim-Christian dialogue, attended among others by the Christian theologian Hans Küng.[52] At a more political level Ayatollah Khomeini has constantly expressed his support of all liberation movements and his sympathy for all the oppressed peoples of the world.

The conception of Islam as an unchanging religion is clearly false. Like all other religions Islam is a living growth, and is thus changing in its actuality, even if its dogmatic formulations do not change. Many Muslims, not all of them liberals, have been aware of ways in which Islamic praxis has changed for the worse. Muḥammad ʿAbduh criticized the excessive reliance of institutions like al-Azhar on the processes of memorizing and of using commentaries, whereas they should have been trying to stimulate creative thinking; and Mawdudi had many scathing remarks to make about about the praxis both of the ulema and of ordinary Muslims.

Hans Küng, who is an eminent Christian theologian, has recently put forward certain views which open up the possibility of having a conception of God's dealing with his world in a way which would give an honoured position to Islam at the side of the other Abrahamic religions. He accepted the view of some earlier scholars that the Christian ideas present in the intellectual milieu of seventh-century Mecca and Arabia were more specifically in the form in which they were held by groups of Christians of Jewish origin, and perhaps by other 'Syrian-Semitic' Christians such as the Nestorians. The way in which such Christians thought about Jesus is closely parallel to the way in which he is presented in the Qur'ān. This is rather different, however, from the way in which he is described in the official ecumenical creeds, which were formulated in the fourth century under the influence of Hellenistic thinking. Hans Küng seems to be asserting that, while the official creed with its Hellenistic bias is to be accepted as true, another more Semitic formulation of the doctrines might be seen as a permissible alternative. The two would be taken as complementary, not as contradicting one another, since in the iconic use of language apparent contradictions are not necessarily real ones. The Qur'ān might then be said to be recalling Christians to aspects of Christian truth which they have been neglecting for centuries.

If this suggestion of the parallel between the Qur'ān and Jewish Christianity is accepted, it would give us a picture of 'salvation history' somewhat as follows. God first chose to reveal something of himself to Abraham, and this was accepted by his son Isaac and his grandson Jacob and supplemented by further revelations, which were preserved by Jacob's descendants the Israelites. The understanding of God and of how he deals with his creatures was extended by further revelations to Moses and the Old Testament prophets. By the time of Jesus certain unsatisfactory features had appeared in Jewish praxis, and through the teaching of Jesus and his sacrificial death these were corrected. Jesus also brought a fuller revelation of God, which was developed by his followers through the working in them of the Holy Spirit. By the time of Muḥammad certain inadequacies had appeared in Christian praxis, and God gave to Muḥammad a revelation which was complementary. Thus Islam may be seen as presenting one facet of the Abrahamic tradition, though not as replacing Judaism and Christianity. This conception of God's pattern of salvation for all humanity can of course be extended to include the other great religions, as well as the lesser religions; but this is not the place for that.

What has to be insisted on is that, if Muslims are to play the creative role in the future world that they are capable of playing, they must adopt a new attitude to other religions. They must see these as having positive achievements to their credit, even if to Muslims they seem far from perfect. Thus the self-image of Islam needs to be modified so that Islam may be perceived as no more than one part of God's plan for the salvation of humanity.

This attitude to other religions should also be extended to other aspects of human culture which are often associated with religion. The non-Muslim observer gains the impression that Islamic traditionalism, by concentrating on religious and moral values, discourages Muslims from paying much attention to the aesthetic aspects even of Islamic culture. Are there any Muslim travel agencies arranging tours to see the gems of Islamic architecture? Muslim rulers and wealthy men certainly appreciated the beauty of many sorts of cultural achievements, but this appreciation does not seem to have been widely shared by Muslims in general. When more Muslims learn to appreciate their own aesthetic heritage, it may be easier for them to appreciate the total human heritage which is open to them.

7 TOWARDS A TRUER SELF-IMAGE

After the critique of the traditional Islamic world-view and self-image in this chapter it might seem to conservative Muslims that it has been completely destroyed; but this is far from being the case. To emphasize this point it may be helpful to specify the outline or skeleton of a truer world-view and self-image.

(a) The Qur'ān provides religious and moral truth revealed by God. Though this was in the first place adapted to the needs of the Arabs of the seventh century, its essentials are of universal validity, and contain guidance for the human race in the twenty-first century and beyond.

(b) Muḥammad was a great prophet and religious leader.

(c) The Islamic religious institution worked out a world-view and self-image, and in this way established a social structure which enabled millions of people to lead a satisfactory life through many centuries. That this now requires to be modified is not because of defects in it as originally formulated for its particular time, but because of modern technological and industrial developments, and of the changes in social structure to which these lead.

(d) The Islamic community has made an important contribution to human history by creating social stability over a great area of the world, even where there were political upheavals.

(e) Islam presents a distinctive version of Abrahamic monotheism, and has thus a place in God's plan for the salvation of humanity. It may possibly become a corrective of certain Christian exaggerations, and may also in co-operation with other religions help to bring about a world in which there is social justice and peace on a basis of sound moral principles.

This is the outline of a truer self-image of Islam than that which is supported by the traditionalists, but it is no more than an outline which has to be filled in by Muslims themselves. Above all what is needed is a renewer or *mujaddid* with the poetic gifts of an Iqbal.

Chapter Six

THE IRANIAN EXPERIENCE

The most dramatic event in the Islamic world this century has been the Iranian revolution of 1978–9 and the overthrow of the Shah. Volumes have been written on the topic from many angles. In the present context the main concern will be to show how the self-image of Iranian Shīʿism differs from that of Sunnite Islam on which the previous chapters have concentrated, and how this self-image has affected the policies of the revolutionary Iranian state. It will be useful, however, to begin with a brief account of the general background of events.

1 SHĪʿISM IN IRAN

Iran is in a unique position in that it is the only Islamic country where the official religion and the religion of the overwhelming majority of the people is Shīʿism, more precisely the Imāmite form of Shīʿism. There is an important body of Imāmite Shīʿites in Iraq, amounting to about half of the population, and smaller groups in the Lebanon, Bahrein and other places. Altogether, however, Imāmite Shīʿites constitute only about 8 per cent of all Muslims in contrast to nearly 90 per cent who are Sunnites. The Imāmites are also known as Twelver Shīʿites (in Arabic Ithnāʿashariyya) because they recognize twelve imams. The other forms of Shīʿism, Zaydism and Ismā'īlism, represented by the Imams of Sanaa in the Yemen and by the Aga Khan's community respectively, form only 2 per cent or 3 per cent of all Muslims, and do not regard themselves as akin to the Imāmites. The common term Shīʿism was found convenient by the Muslim writers on sects.

The basic belief of all the forms of Shīʿism is that the rightful successor of Muḥammad as 'imam' (leader) of all the Muslims was his cousin and son-in-law ʿAlī. The effective successor of Muḥammad in 632, however, with the title of 'caliph' (successor, deputy), was Abū-Bakr, one of his oldest supporters, and he was followed by two others, ʿUmar and ʿUthmān. ʿAlī eventually became fourth caliph in 656 and ruled until his assassination in 661. The Shīʿites hold that the rightful successor of ʿAlī was his son Ḥasan, who made an ineffectual attempt to claim the caliphate in 661 and then retired from politics, and that the rightful successor after him was his brother Ḥusayn. On the death of the first Umayyad caliph in 680 Ḥusayn claimed the caliphate in opposition to the caliph's son Yazīd, but he gained little support, and his gallant band of just over a hundred, mostly members of 'the family' (of Muḥammad), was massacred at Kerbela when they refused to surrender to a large army sent against them by Yazīd. This martyrdom of Ḥusayn, as they consider it, is still commemorated annually by the Imāmites and stirs up deep religious emotions among ordinary people.

A contemporary Shīʿite thinker, S. Husain M. Jafri, who accepts Western historico-critical methods, has given an impressive presentation of the Imāmite case in his book *The Origins and Early Development of Shi'a Islam.*[1] He sees the appointment of Abū-Bakr as caliph in 632 in place of ʿAlī as a preference for a purely human candidate to one who could rely on the divine inspiration which had clearly been given to Muḥammad's clan of Hāshim. Somewhat similarly he sees the Umayyad caliphate, and especially the accession of Yazīd, as a reasssertion of Arab conservatism against 'Muḥammad's progressive Islamic *action*'. It would have been unthinkable for a grandson of the Prophet to acknowledge the worldly Yazīd as caliph.

> In order to acknowledge this *reaction* against Islamic *action*, Ḥusayn prepared his strategy. In his opinion he had the right, by virtue of his family and his own position therein, to guide his people and revive their respect. However, if this right were challenged, he was willing to sacrifice and die for his cause. He realized that mere force of arms would not have saved Islamic *action* and consciousness. To him it needed a shaking and jolting of hearts and feelings. This, he decided, could only be achieved through sacrifice and sufferings.

Thus the death of Ḥusayn was the death of one bearing witness to a high ideal, regardless of cost. This is the faith which supports the self-sacrifice of so many young Iranians.

According to the Imāmites the rightful imam after Ḥusayn was his son, and then the imamate descended from father to son until the twelfth imam. None of these imams made claims publicly, and they were able to live peacefully under the Umayyad caliphs (until 750) and then under the ʿAbbāsid caliphs. The Eleventh Imam died on or about 1 January 874, leaving a son who mysteriously disappeared either then or a few years later. The Imāmites claim that he had not died but had gone into 'occultation' (*ghayba*, literally 'absence'). For some seventy years he always had an 'agent' (*wakīl*) in the Imāmite community who was in touch with him; and this is known as the period of the 'lesser occultation'. In 940 the series of 'agents' came to an end, and this marks the beginning of the 'greater occultation' during which the community has no contact with the Hidden Imam. The Imāmites believe, however, that he is still alive and that at an appropriate time he will return to set things right in the world. The Hidden Imam is also known as the 'guided one' or Mahdi, a kind of Messiah-figure. This special belief of the Imāmites has influenced political events in Iran at various points.

For some six centuries the Imāmite Shīʿites were scattered throughout the Islamic lands in small groups, and included Arabs as well as Iranians. A great change was brought about in 1501 when a leader, later known as Shah Ismāʿīl, conquered much of Iran and made Imāmism the official religion. This led gradually to a concentration of Imāmites in Iran, apart from the large body in Iraq where there were important Imāmite shrines, and a few smaller groups in other localities; at the same time the Sunnites in Iran faded out. Iran also became a centre for Imāmite scholarship, and there were developments in the fields of law and theology. The dynasty founded by Shah Ismāʿīl, the Safavids, continued to rule Iran until 1722, and by that date Imāmism was well established. The rest of the eighteenth century was an unsettled period with occupation by Afghan war-lords and the rule of the Sunnite Nader Shah (1736–47), but Imāmism remained the dominant religion. The Qājār dynasty, which came to power towards the end of the century and continued until 1924, needed the support of the Imāmite scholars and in return supported them.

Imāmite Shīʿism has an image of itself which differs from that of Sunnism in important ways. It regards itself as alone the true Islam, since the Sunnites fell into error when they accepted Abū-Bakr and rejected ʿAlī as the rightful successor to Muḥammad; but in recent decades there have been attempts to bring Shīʿism and Sunnism closer together. A distinctive feature of the Imāmites is that they are looking forward to the return of the Mahdi, and in the meantime it is a kind of temporary measure that they follow the teaching of their Imams as interpreted by the ulema. Actually their form of the Sharīʿa differs only slightly from that of the standard Sunnite schools, but they base their detailed laws on their own collections of Ḥadīth, which are backed by the authority of Imams. The Imāmites think of themselves as distinguished by their loyalty to the house of the Prophet, and, as mentioned already, each year they commemorate with mourning rites the martyrdom of his grandson Ḥusayn at Kerbela. The latter, because of his brave acceptance of suffering and death, has come to be regarded as having special powers as an intercessor, and in popular religion he is appealed to to help suppliants to obtain what they need, materially and spiritually.

The self-image of Iranian Islam has been influenced by the millennium-old dualism of the Iranians, expressed in the Zoroastrian religion, in Manichaeism and in sectarian Mazdakism. The extent of this influence is debated by scholars.[2] Islam, of course, is strictly monotheistic, but it has a place for the Devil or Satan, usually called Iblīs in the Qur'ān. Some small early Islamic sects in Iran emphasized dualistic ideas. Within Islam the poet Ferdausi in his epic the *Shahnameh* created an image of Iran as the people of purity and truth, confronting Turan, the evil of savagery and barbarism pressing on Iran from Central Asia in the shape of Turkish tribes. This was a national rather than a religious self-image, but at the heart of Iranian Shīʿism is the figure of Ḥusayn, the pure and upright, struggling against the powers of evil represented by the armies of Yazīd. Indeed, Iranian Shīʿism regards itself as the citadel of truth and light holding out against the error, darkness and evil of the Sunnites formerly, and now of the superpowers and not least of the 'great Satan' of the United States.

Though much of the Sunnite world-view and self-image is shared by the Imāmite Shīʿites, there are also subtle differences. There is less emphasis on unchangingness, since worldly conditions will be changed for the better when the Mahdi appears. Similarly, while Islam already has supreme truth, something further is possible with the coming of the Mahdi. There is the same idealization of Islamic life under Muḥammad himself and under ʿAlī, but there are criticisms of life under the first three caliphs. There is not the same emphasis as among Sunnites on Dār al-Islām, doubtless because of the restricted numbers and geographical distribution of the Shīʿites, though of course, as just noted, the Iranian Shīʿites see themselves as the bearers of divine truth and light.

2 THE IRANIAN RELIGIOUS INSTITUTION

The doctrinal differences between Sunnism and Imāmite Shīʿism affected the form and powers of the religious institution associated with each. When Sunnism was taking definite shape about the year 900, the religious institution or body of ulema was seen as deriving its authority from the caliph (who was sometimes also called imam); and this continued to be the case after the caliphs lost all political power in 945, since the effective rulers, though actually maintaining themselves by their armies, were nominally appointees of the caliph. Even after 1258, when the caliphate to all intents and purposes ceased to exist, religious institutions in Sunnite countries remained dependent on the rulers. The later claim of the Ottoman sultans to be caliphs, though widely accepted by Sunnites, had little practical effect outside the Ottoman empire. Within the empire the religious institution was largely dependent on the caliph-sultan.

After his conquest of Iran Shah Ismāʿīl invited Shīʿite ulema from other regions to come there, and these were of course dependent on him. Gradually, however, they established themselves as an essential feature of the state. They alone could preside in the Sharīʿa courts, though there were also other customary-law courts in which they took no part. There was a rudimentary religious institution, since the ulema had a representative at court known as the Sadr, and it was he who nominated the chief jurisconsult with the title of Shaykh al-Islām. With the growing power of the religious institution there developed arguments about the extent to which Ijtihād is permissible, that is, whether in a novel situation suitably qualified contemporary ulema may apply the principles of the Sharīʿa in a fresh way. Towards the year 1600 a school of jurisprudence emerged which wanted to restrict the right of making new adaptations of the Sharīʿa and to oblige ulema to follow only the decisions of the Imams as these were to be found in the reports (*akhbār*) transmitted from them. This was known as the Akhbārī school, and was dominant at the time of the fall of the Safavids (1722) and for most of the eighteenth century.

The period from the fall of the Safavids to the attainment of power by the Qājārs at the end of the century was a difficult one for the Imāmite scholars, since Iran suffered from Afghan invaders and rulers who mostly had Sunnite sympathies and deprived the Imāmite ulema of some of their privileges. In the later eighteenth century, however, a new school appeared among the Imāmites in Iraq known as the Uṣūlī school. It held that certain of the ulema had the right of Ijtihād, and also that ordinary Muslims ought to imitate or follow the decisions of *mujtahids* (those practising Ijtihād) as well as those of the Imams; indeed each Muslim should choose a *mujtahid* to follow. Under the Qājār Shahs the Uṣūlī school became dominant, and the ulema recovered most of the powers and privileges they had lost.

Towards the middle of the nineteenth century a further development took place. It was realized that one *mujtahid* could be wiser and more learned than another, and therefore more worthy to be imitated or followed; and from this it was a short step to the idea that there should be a single 'source for imitation' (*marjaʿ-e taqlīd*) with authority to give formal legal opinions (*fatvas*) binding on all Imāmites. The first to be widely, though not universally, recognized as *marjaʿ-e taqlīd* was a Shaykh Muḥammad Ḥasan who lived at Nejef in Iraq and died in 1850. He was succeeded by an Iranian Shaykh Mortaza Ansari (1800–64) who was more generally recognized. Since his death there has not always been a single *marjaʿ* – the last was Ayatollah Borujerdi who died in 1961 – but sometimes a group of senior ulema has been recognized as being 'sources for imitation' jointly.

The concept of *taqlīd*, commonly rendered 'imitation' in this context, is more precisely the acting in accordance with the rulings of the *mujtahid* one has chosen to imitate or follow. What is implied in this was worked out in considerable detail by Mortaza Ansari, and his thought formed the basis for the structuring and organization of the religious institution in an informal hierarchy. Above the rank and file of the ulema (often called mollahs in Iran) were the *mujtahids*, of whom some seniors came to be called Ayatollahs and, in outstanding cases, great Ayatollahs. (Ayatollah means 'sign of God'.) Sometimes there was a supreme 'source of imitation' at the top of the pyramid. This grading was reached by a kind of informal consensus. The final result was that by 1978 the Ayatollahs had in their hands a powerful institution which could disseminate their thinking and their commands rapidly throughout the country.

At the same time there came to be a wide acceptance of the view maintained by the ulema that they alone, by their knowledge of the Qur'ān, the Ḥadīth and the teaching of the Imams, could interpret for their contemporaries the mind of the Hidden Imams. From this it followed that the possession of military power did not give the right to rule. Rule was only legitimized when the ruler acted in accordance with the teachings of the religious institution. All other rule was usurpation. This belief in the Hidden Imam was taken to imply that the religious institution was above the actual ruler. The implication was to some extent admitted by the Qājār dynasty since they needed the support of the religious institution. This did not mean, however, that the rulers always did what the ulema wanted. During the nineteenth century the Qājārs took some steps to modernize their country in minor ways, and this policy was opposed by the ulema because they feared it would lead to a reduction of their own power. In so far as the poor and the bazaaris or bazaar traders were also affected, the ulema were able to gain a reputation as the defenders of ordinary people against oppressive rulers.

There were one or two outstanding cases where the ulema were successful in their opposition to the government. The Shahs, in order to finance their imports from Europe and their travels there, gave concessions to Europeans, who, for example, gained the right to collect a certain tax on payment of a lump sum to the Shah. In 1872 a wide-ranging concession was given to a British subject, Baron de Reuter, which adversely affected the bazaaris in particular, and they and the ulema together eventually managed to get the concession cancelled. Something similar happened in 1891, when a Tobacco Monopoly (for the marketing of all tobacco grown in Iran) was given to another British subject. On this occasion the 'source of imitation' of the time, Ayatollah Shirazi, published a declaration that it was unlawful in the current circumstances for believers to use tobacco or to deal in it; and this was so widely obeyed by the people in general that the Monopoly had to be cancelled. The ulema also played a part in the constitutional movement of 1905 to 1911, but they were by no means the only factor and probably not the most important.

The coming to power of Reza Khan, as prime minister in 1921, and then as Reza Shah on the ousting of the Qājārs in 1924, led to a serious deterioration in the power of the religious institution. Up to that time modernization had amounted to little more than the import of Western comforts and luxuries for the wealthy, and little had been done by way of developing the country. This was in large part due to the rivalry of Great Britain and Russia for control of Iran. In 1907 they had made an agreement by which the northern third of the country was a Russian sphere of influence, and the southern third a British sphere, while the central third was open to both. It suited them, however, to keep the country largely undeveloped. Reza Shah had thus open to him wide possibilities for speeding up modernization, and he set about this energetically. Western-type education was encouraged; new laws were made, not based on the Sharīʿa, and new courts established to administer these; various welfare services were secularized. While such changes in themselves weakened the religious institution, there were other measures which increased government control over it. More and more the ulema became opponents of the Pahlevi regime.

Reza Shah was doubtless well aware of the policies of Mustafa Kemal Atatürk in Turkey and how he had made the country a 'laic' state and demolished the religious institution in order to facilitate the process of modernization. The very choice of 'Pahlevi' for the name of the dynasty suggests an interest in glorifying the pre-Islamic past of Iran at the expense of Islam. The glorification of the past was continued even more energetically under his son, Mohammad Reza Shah, and culminated in the grandiose celebration of the 2500th anniversary of the Iranian monarchy in 1971. Naturally this also was regarded by the religious institution and by many other Muslims as an attack on Islam.

3 THE PREPARATION FOR REVOLUTION

There have been many analyses of the situation in Iran which led to the success of the revolution and the downfall of the Shah. There is wide agreement that the root cause was the rapidity with which the Shah was able to pursue his modernizing policies after the great increase in his oil revenues. To make modernization possible he created a large Western-educated class, and this class expected that it would share in much of the material culture of the West. The prosperity of this class naturally led to widespread discontent in those sections of the community which had little or no share in the new wealth. There were increasing numbers of poor people, unemployed or only partly employed, in the shanty towns round the cities. In 1963 in the so-called 'White Revolution' a million and a half peasant families had obtained land, but this had in part been offset by agricultural stagnation and general inflation, so that sections of the rural population were also discontented. Other groups became hostile to the Shah when in 1975, in order to strengthen his position, he established a single Resurgence Party and tried to weaken the religious institution. These measures antagonized the bazaaris or small merchants. The more powerful Westernized business community was next alienated by being blamed for inflation and by the enacting of measures to stop profiteering. Reductions in the wages of oil and factory workers turned them against the Shah; and many of the Western-educated middle class were finding life difficult because of inflation. When all these disaffected groups were brought together with the common purpose of ousting the Shah, his expulsion was almost inevitable.

There was much intellectual activity in Iran in the 1960s and 1970s among both ulema and others. There was wide agreement that the root of the troubles was modernization or Westernization, or at least some aspects of that. People began to speak of a disease which they called 'occidentosis' or 'Westoxication' (*gharbzadeghe*), and a book with this title was published by Jalal Al-e Ahmad in 1962.[3] This was, of course, a more sophisticated way of describing the danger, felt by Muslims everywhere, of losing their Islamic identity. It is generally agreed that the decisive thinker who made the revolution possible was Ali Shariati (1933–77). As a student at the university of Meshhed his political activities led to a spell in prison, but he gained his bachelor's degree in 1959 and a scholarship to Paris, where he eventually obtained a doctorate in sociology in 1964. Among intellectuals whom he met in Paris were Franz Fanon, whose book *The Wretched of the Earth* he translated into Persian, as well as other supporters of the Algerian liberation movement. On his return to Iran in 1965 by claiming that his subject was 'Islamic sociology' he was able, despite government measures against him, to go on lecturing to students, first in Meshhed, then in Tehran until 1973. After that he was virtually silenced by imprisonment and house arrest, though tapes and mimeographed copies of his lectures circulated. He was especially popular with the Westernized youth.

Shariati was above all an orator who could move audiences by his flamboyant style of lecturing. Although he had a doctorate, his works were not scientifically argued, as critics have noted. The following amusing passage may be given as an example of his style:

> Then Jesus (peace be upon him) appeared. He abrogated Judaism and overthrew the Roman Empire. However, Caesar changed his name to Pope, the Jewish rabbis were replaced by Christian monks, the old Roman senators became clergymen and Vatican cardinals, the palace was called the church and Jupiter acted like Jesus.[4]

This is much less fanciful than might at first appear, since he is using historical names for contemporary realities. What he is asserting is that, even when there are great changes in names and ideas, the holders of power continue to hold power; and he is possibly here thinking chiefly of the Iranian religious institution which he saw as unable to act effectively against oppression. In Paris he came to feel that all the liberation movements of the Third World were struggling against the same colonialist and neocolonialist oppressors. He thought that the true Islam was committed to working for social justice by opposing all oppressive forces; and he gave this an Islamic basis by using the Qur'ānic term 'oppressed' (*mostazʿafin, mustaḍʿafin*) and by calling Muslims to their traditional duty of 'commanding the good and forbidding the evil'.

With this last point was closely linked the distinction he drew between what we called 'Safavid Shīʿism' and 'Alid Shīʿism'. In a book on this subject he tabulated the differences under eight heads.[5] The most important point was his rejection of the traditional view that ordinary Muslims should be passive politically as they waited for the Hidden Imam; instead they should be ready to follow the guidance of 'conscientious, responsible, pure men representing the leadership of the Imam' and to work for the attainment of social justice and other reforms. Those who could thus give guidance were not the offical ulema, whom he criticized severely, but 'enlightened thinkers' (*raushanfekran*). The activities to which their guidance would lead were not simply on behalf of the poor and oppressed in Iran but for similar people throughout the world. Along with this went a new understanding of the proto-martyr Ḥusayn. No longer was he merely the Intercessor who could help one to endure suffering; he was the great exemplar, fighting and sacrificing his life not merely for the restoration of the rule of the Prophet's family, but for the cause of social justice to oppressed peoples throughout the world.[6]

Because of his popularity as a speaker Shariati seems to have played a major role in the creation of a new self-image of Islam as activist and indeed revolutionary. In this way he brought many of the Western-educated middle class to regard Islam as a focus for action against the Shah. He was often criticized by the ulema - not unnaturally in the light of his attacks on them – but some of them came to understand the value and importance of his activist presentation of Islam. Because this presentation had the figure of Ḥusayn at its centre, it also was attractive to various groups of more traditionalist Muslims. In a sense Shariati's work had been completed before his imprisonment in 1973, and his premature death in 1977 led, if anything, to an increase in his influence.

The man who managed to bring together all the opposition forces in a drive to expel the Shah was Ayatollah Ruhollah Musavi Khomeini. Born in 1902, he went to Qom in 1921 to complete his studies, and in 1926 attained the rank of *mujtahid*. As early as 1944 he was engaged in public criticism of aspects of the Pahlevi regime, but it was during the wave of unrest in 1962 and 1963 that he came to the fore as an outspoken critic. In consequence he was exiled, first to Turkey, then in 1965 to Nejef in Iraq, and finally in 1978 to Paris. During this period his thought took shape as he expounded it in lectures to students. He was deeply concerned with the problems of alienation or the loss of a distinctive Islamic identity as a result of the impact of the West. To counteract this 'occidentosis' he held that it was necessary to create a milieu in which the Sharīʿa was dominant and in which there was ideological uniformity. Although he was one of the ulema, he came to share Shariati's conception of Shīʿite Islam as activist:

> Islam is the religion of militant individuals who are committed to truth and justice. It is the religion of those who desire independence. It is the school of those who struggle against imperialism.[7]

The true Islam, which had existed under Muḥammad, ʿAlī and Ḥusayn, was a world-wide movement to secure social justice for the oppressed. Khomeini, however, did not leave leadership vaguely in the hands of 'enlightened thinkers' as Shariati had done, but agreed that it should be in the hands of members of the religious institution. This was his principle of 'the rule of the jurist' (*velayat-e faqīh*). (The word *velayat* has a range of meanings, and other translations are used; but 'rule' appears to be his primary meaning.) Though this principle was in some respects a new departure, it also had deep roots in Shī'ite thought. It had been commonly held that in the absence of the Imam those best qualified to guide the community were the jurists, and that an actual ruler was only legitimate in so far as he followed the rulings of the jurists. From this it was a short step to the view that the jurists should have governmental responsibility. Perhaps the idea of there being a single supreme 'source of imitation' may have come in here, since it is noteworthy that the principle is formulated as 'the rule of the jurist' (in the singular).

By 1978 Ayatollah Khomeini was in a position to play a leading role in the movement against the Shah. He showed his political skill by denouncing all the defects and objectionable features of the government, while remaining largely silent about his positive programme. In this way he was able to bring in groups that were secular or left-wing and get them to co-operate with the traditionalist Muslim groupings. Eventually the Shah decided to leave, and Khomeini returned and was able to take control of the government.

4 THE REVOLUTIONARY SELF-IMAGE

Ayatollah Khomeini and his supporters have achieved much more than most people thought possible when they first came to power in 1979. They have kept the country functioning as a modern state, and seem to have effected improvements at certain points, such as the supply of rural electricity. They waged a long and bitter war against Iraq and repelled attempts to occupy their territory. This has been so because the religious leaders or jurists directing national policies have managed to retain the co-operation of politicians, civil servants, and other persons with Western skills. This is not the place to assess the successes and failures of the Khomeini regime, but only to look at the effect of the religious self-image in its 'revolutionary' form on various aspects of the conduct of affairs.

One of the obvious features of the new regime, as it has been an aim of the Islamic resurgence everywhere, has been the restoration of Islamic forms of life, such as the banning of alcohol and the insistence on the *chador* for women. It may be noted, however, that, although women had to wear the *chador* and were banned from some occupations, such as engineering, there does not seem to have been any attempt to reintroduce the strict segregation of women and to confine them to domestic duties. On the contrary, women have played a part in the armed forces, and semi-official sources have spoken about the need, after the end of the war, for women's labour to help in the rebuilding of the country, at least in industry.

These are aspects of Khomeini's demand for the creation of a milieu dominated by the Sharīʿa but there are other aspects which are open to more serious criticisms. In the 1940s, besides speaking against the Pahlevi regime, and objecting to the existing methods of administering justice, he was advocating a return to the more rapid and less time-consuming methods of Islamic justice, as well as to the traditional penalties. In the course of 1979 hundreds of opponents of the revolution were condemned to death after extremely short trials, and there were also many executions at some later periods. Much use was made of a Qur'ānic verse which prescribed death and torture for 'those who fought against God and his Messenger and actively spread corruption in the land' (5.35). The provisions of Shīʿite law to ensure fair trials seem to have been forgotten or set aside.

The reassertion of Islamic values tends to be limited to those values embodied in the traditional self-image as the ordinary Iranian Muslim understands it. The ideal Islamic community is what is supposed to have existed under Muḥammad, 'Alī and Ḥusayn. Despite the claim that many of the Shī'ite ulema have the right of Ijtihād little was done before the revolution, and little seems to have been done since, to adapt the formulations of the Sharīʿa to contemporary circumstances. The Ayatollahs and *mujtahids* have not been interested in general social reforms, though some small changes may have been forced upon the ruling élite by the responsibilities of government.

Despite formulations of human rights in Islam by such bodies as the Organization of the Islamic Conference, and even some discussion by Shīʿite jurists, concern for human rights is no part of the Islamic consciousness of the ordinary Iranian Muslim (any more than it is of ordinary Muslims elsewhere), and consequently there have been many infringements of what non-Muslims regard as basic human rights. The disregard of diplomatic immunities, as in the affair of the American hostages, is a minor example of this limitation of the Islamic consciousness. More serious is the treatment of dissenters from the traditional world-view. Ayatollah Khomeini spoke of the need for ideological unity or uniformity; and various happenings make one wonder whether the jurists consider the death penalty appropriate for those who do not conform. Or is it only inflicted if they are also held to be a danger to the state? When Sir Hamilton Gibb spoke of what he called 'Mahdism' (which was not confined to Shīʿites), he maintained that 'the heresy of Mahdism is its belief not only that the minds and wills of men can be dominated by force, but that truth can be demonstrated by the edge of the sword'.[8] One is inclined to ask to what extent the Iranian religious leaders subscribe to this belief. Events appear to show that it is widely accepted by their followers.

In fairness it should also be noted that non-Muslims may also believe in something like the 'heresy' of Mahdism. For example, some aspects of United States policy in the Gulf in the latter half of 1987 look as if they were based on the idea that the minds and wills of men can be dominated by force, even if truth cannot be demonstrated by the sword. One wonders how the Americans can hope for success by such policies when they are confronted by opponents who are utterly convinced of the sublimity of martyrdom because they are bearing witness to a lofty principle against overwhelming force.

Another aspect of the new activist Iranian self-image is that it gives a central place to the conception of Islam as a struggle for truth and justice against falsehood and evil. An American woman anthropologist, who was researching in an Iranian village from June 1978 to December 1979, found that the villagers had accepted with enthusiasm the new conception of Ḥusayn as one who was fighting against a godless tyrant and knew that his martyrdom would be an example for all future ages:

> Because he actively chose to face death and worldly defeat in order to become a *shahid* (meaning both martyr and witness) of Islam for all times, Husain and his martyrdom . . . have become the central paradigm of Shi'i Islam. In this view of Islam, all human history is pictured as a continuous struggle

> between the forces of evil and the forces of good. In every age, villagers told me, there is a Husain, a man who fights on the side of God, and a Yazid, who fights against God.[9]

Unlike Sunnite Muslims, however, the Shīʿites do not see themselves as the sole upholders of good against evil. Doubtless this is because they are fewer in numbers – only a tenth or twelfth of the Sunnites – and mostly live in only a small area of the globe. Ayatollah Khomeini as well as Shariati saw liberation movements throughout the world as engaged in the same struggle, and so as potential allies. Thus Iran may be said to be making a bid for the leadership of the Third World in its struggle against the First World. The Iranian leaders, too, seem to realize that there is a difference between the kind of Christian who supports liberation theology, and the nominal Western Christian who does not criticize the economic and political activities of the 'great Satan' which in Muslim eyes is the heart of the evil and corruption they are struggling against.

Prominent among these forms of evil is the present regime in Iraq. President Saddam Hussein is not only seen with justification as an aggressor, but he and the ruling élite are also held to be infidels and apostates. Others might rather call them nominal Muslims, minimal in their observance of distinctive Islamic practice. It is known, for example, that at gatherings such as university receptions all but a handful of the Iraqis present will be drinking whisky. Just as it would have been unthinkable for the Imam Ḥusayn to come to terms with the infidel and apostate Yazīd, so it is extremely difficult for Ayatollah Khomeini to make peace with Iraq. The example of Imam Ḥusayn's readiness to sacrifice his life witnessing to a principle, though he had no hope of success, plays a part here. This is one of the points at which the Shīʿite self-image differs from the Sunnite, for Sunnite ulema held that the Jihād was only to be pursued where there was some chance of victory.

Chapter Seven

EPILOGUE

After this examination of Islamic fundamentalism some reflections on the present position are in order.

It would appear that the basic question which is demanding an answer from all Muslims is whether they want to be part of the One World, or to go it alone and live in a purely Islamic world of their own. It is obvious, of course, that the greater majority of Muslims want to have all the material comforts and luxuries produced in the West, but many traditionalists think they can have these and yet remain insulated from other aspects of Western culture, which they see as decadent in themselves and as corrupting Islamic society. This attitude has deep roots in Islamic history. From the third and fourth Islamic centuries the ulema have been using totalitarian methods to ensure the absolute dominance of the traditional world-view. The religious institution of the Ottoman empire thought that it could preserve the world-view intact by paying no attention to new intellectual currents in Western Europe, and preventing the inhabitants of the empire from learning about them; and there are still groups of reactionary ulema who try to carry out a policy of this kind.

What makes such a policy impossible is a relatively simple fact. Presumably the Muslims would not want to be mere parasites on the West, buying Western products but having no share in producing them. If, however, there are to be Muslim experts in the natural and social sciences and in technological industry, they will inevitably acquire something of the general intellectual outlook of the West and will begin to ask questions to which the traditional Islamic world-view, despite its claim to rationality, provides no answers. This is hard fact. If Muslims want to have a share in the world scientific movement, they cannot shut themselves away in the fortress of their medieval world-view, but must see themselves as part of a greater world in which there is much of value. One would indeed expect that Muslims would want to share, not only in world science, but in the whole intellectual and cultural life of the human race. This is our heritage as human beings living in one world.

If Muslims continue to think in terms of the duality of Dār al-Islām and Dār al-Ḥarb, and assume that the former is or will soon become the larger part of the duality, it may seem satisfactory to go on living in Dār al-Islām and neglecting the rest of the world. The actuality is, however, that Muslims are only about one-fifth of the human race, and that there are no signs of impending large-scale conversions to Islam among the other four-fifths. Thus Muslims who shut themselves off from what is happening in the greater part of the world are in fact making a kind of ghetto for themselves. To be aware of what is happening in the rest of the world is not necessarily to approve of it. Many traditionalist Muslims, however, almost completely ignorant of religious and philanthropic movements in the rest of the world, have tended to assume that these are all worthless. The earlier studies by Muslims of other religions mostly looked for the points at which their doctrines could be classified as heretical. One of the things that should now specially concern Muslims is a study of other religions in order to see what there is of positive value in them. In this way they may come to realize that the rest of the world is not full of people who must be fought against, but contains many with whom they could co-operate in the pursuit of shared ends.

This is one facet of the most important change which is needed in the outlook of Muslims, namely, an openness to all historical truth. As Sir Hamilton Gibb noted,[1] Islamic thought lost its flexibility after the fourth Islamic century and became petrified, and this was largely because the historians, instead of maintaining the autonomy of their discipline, allowed themselves to be dictated to by the needs of theological dogma as expressed by the ulema. Yet, if the course of history is determined by God, as Muslims hold, it becomes a mark of unbelief to substitute what one imagines God to have done for what he really did, or in other words to substitute a theological rewriting of history for the objective facts (what God really did) as these may be discovered by the methods of the critical historian.

One of the important points at which this 'unbelieving' and unhistorical self-image of Islam affects contemporary events is in the idealization of early Islam, when it is regarded as a perfect society to which a return is possible and desirable; no such return can solve our contemporary problems. Moreover no amount of idealization can conceal the fact that in the time of Muḥammad Arabia was only beginning to emerge from a barbaric past. It may be correct to say that Islam was attempting to overcome that past barbarism, but traces of it remain in early Muslim practice and are sanctioned by the Qur'ān. Examples are the torture of opponents, when captured, by cutting off a hand and a foot (5.33), and the amputation of a hand as a punishment for theft (5.38). It was presumably such verses that Fazlur Rahman had in mind when he said that new ethical and legal formulations should not be based on isolated verses but on the teaching of the Qur'ān as a whole. Human beings in a mature civilization cannot accept such practices of the distant past as an ideal to be followed.

The unhistorical self-image also impoverishes the lives of Muslims in other ways. V. S. Naipaul in his book *Among the Believers*[2] has a chapter entitled 'Killing History' in which he describes how traditional teaching of history consists in the glorification of one or two periods and neglect of the rest – all this with a view to encouraging today's Muslims to be like the early Arabs in following the Qur'ān. Some school textbooks he looked into had hardly anything between an idealized picture of the period up to the death of ʿAlī and the lives of Iqbal and Mr Jinnah; and he concludes that such history leads to unreality. In order to play their part adequately in the modern world Muslims should not merely have a wide and realistic knowledge of the main events in Islamic history, but also know something of the long processes by which the rest of the world has come to be as it is.

Another area in which Muslims need to work hard if they are to take a full share in the life of the One World is in the expansion and reformulation of the Sharīʿa. It is claimed that the Sharīʿa gives moral guidance for every aspect of human life, and it may be allowed that it did in fact cover a large part of medieval life; but there has been little done to adapt it to the new social structures of life at the end of the twentieth century. In this field, in addition to a need for the reformulation of 'the principles of jurisprudence' (*uṣūl al-fiqh*), it is necessary for Muslim jurists to realize how much they have in common with non-Muslim jurists and to work together with these on a fuller moral basis for the United Nations and on other aspects of international life. The differences between Muslims and non-Muslims on the details of human rights should not blind Muslims to the need for taking steps to ensure that the human rights acknowledged by Muslims are in fact observed in Islamic countries. For this it is necessary to have an awakening of the public Muslim consciousness to the importance of human rights and the establishment of bodies to monitor the observance of rights in Muslim countries.

Such a programme for the correction of the faulty self-image of Islam may seem utopian and unlikely to be realized. Yet there are some contrary factors which should be noted. Some of the ulema are beginning to show more liberal tendencies, and there is, of course, a large, mainly silent, body of liberal opinion in Islam. When ordinary Muslims become aware that the idyllic conditions they were promised if they went back to early Islam are unlikely to be realized in practice, there may be a great revulsion of feeling against those who advocated that policy. In the contemporary intellectual and cultural turmoil there is much life beneath the surface, and from this might burst out new initiatives which could completely transform the scene. That at least is the outcome for which the believer in God, Muslim or non-Muslim, should be praying.

GLOSSARY

ʿAbbāsids dynasty of caliphs ruling from Baghdad from 750 to 1258, but without power after 945.

Ashʿarites the main school of 'philosophical theology'.

Awqāf (Turkish *Evkaf*), plural of *waqf*, q.v.

caliph (Arabic *khalīfa*, successor, deputy) – title of head of Islamic state after Muḥammad. From 632 to 661, the four 'rightly guided' (*rāshidūn*) caliphs; from 661 to 750 the Umayyads; from 750 to 1258 the ʿAbbāsids. The Ottoman sultans latterly claimed they had inherited the caliphate from the ʿAbbāsids, but it was abolished by the Turkish Republic in 1924. See p.89f.

Companions Muslims who had known Muḥammad and thus could be sources of Ḥadīth about him; the names of some 10,000 are recorded.

Dār al-Ḥarb the house or sphere of war; that is, those regions of the earth not under Islamic rule.

Dār al-Islām the house or sphere of Islam, that is, those regions ruled by a Muslim and observing the Sharīʿa.

Ḥadīth anecdotes about something Muḥammad said or did, used for legal purposes; formerly called 'traditions'; the collections of Ḥadīth are vast.

Hijra the emigration of Muḥammad from Mecca to Medina in AD 622.

Ijtihād the use of independent judgment by a jurist, implying the basing of a legal rule on first principles.

Imāmites the group of Shīʿites also known as Twelvers; see pp.125–8.

Jāhiliyya the time of ignorance or barbarism; that is, Arabia before Islam.

Jihād 'holy war', but basically means expenditure of effort and can apply to spiritual struggle.

Kalām 'philosophical (or rational) theology'.

madrasa (Turkish *medrese*), a college primarily for jurisprudence.

Mahdī the 'guided one', a messianic personage; see p.101.

Muftī one authorised to give a *fatwā*, judicial opinion.

mujaddid a 'renewer' of religion.

Muʿtazilites an important school of 'philosophical theologians', generally regarded as heretical.

Ottoman empire the state created by the Ottoman Turks in Asia Minor and SE Europe from the fourteenth century; after 1453 the capital was Istanbul.

Quraysh the Arab tribe inhabiting Mecca.

Rāshidūn the first four 'rightly guided' caliphs.

Razzia a tribal raid, often with the objective of seizing camels.

Sharīʿa the law (comparable to the Jewish Torah) given by God through Qur'ān and Ḥadīth.

Shīʿites a group of Islamic sects; see pp.125f. Often used to refer only to the Imāmite Shīʿites of Iran, etc.

Sīra the biography of Muḥammad.

Sunna the example of Muḥammad as a legal and moral norm; it is known from the Ḥadīth.

Sunnites the main body of Muslims (about 90 per cent); incorrectly called 'orthodox'; see p.28.

ulema Muslim religious scholars, basically jurists; see p.27f.

Umayyads dynasty of caliphs ruling from Damascus 661–750.

umma the community of Muslims.

waqf a religious trust, plural *awqāf*, Turkish *evkaf*.

NOTES

CHAPTER I THE TRADITIONAL SELF-IMAGE OF ISLAM

1 E.g. Mohammed Arkoun, *Pour une critique de la raison islamique*, Paris, 1984, pp.58f.
2 *Islamochristiana*, xii (1986), 159.
3 See below, Ch.V, 2a, p.80.
4 Cf. *Risalat al-Jihad*, no.36 (Sept. 1985), p.77.
5 H9. R. Idris in *Orientalia Hispanica*, ed. J. M. Barral, Leiden, 1974, vol i, p.405.
6 See pp.58–60. below.
7 See also W. Montgomery Watt, *Muhammad's Mecca*, Edinburgh, 1988, Ch.2, 4d.
8 Abū Dāwūd, *Sunan*, vol.ii, p.101, and in other Muslim writers. See also L. Massignon, *Opera Minora*, Beirut, 1963, vol i, pp.92–6.
9 References in W. Montgomery Watt, 'Created in his Image', *Transactions of the Glasgow University Oriental Society*, xviii (1959–60), pp.38–49.
10 G. H. A. Juynboll, *The Authenticity of the Tradition Literature: Discussions in Modern Egypt*, Leiden, 1969, pp.121–38.
11 H. A. R. Gibb, *Modern Trends in Islam*, Chicago, 1947, p.64.
12 Fazlur Rahman, *Islam and Modernity: Transformation of an Intellectual Tradition*, Chicago, 1982, p.38.
13 Bernard Lewis, *The Muslim Discovery of Europe*, London, 1982.
14 *Risalat al-Jihad*, no. 48.
15 See *Encyclopaedia of Islam*[2], article Ahl al-Ṣuffa.
16 Gibb, *Modern Trends*, p.125.

17 Th. Nöldeke, F. Schwally, *Geschichte des Qorāns*, Leipzig, 1909 (2nd edn) vol.i, pp.248–51.

18 W. Montgomery Watt, *Muhammad at Medina*, Oxford, 1956, pp.378–85, quoting al-Bukhārī, 67.37.1 and other material.

19 *Deuteronomy* 22.22; *Leviticus* 20.10.

20 *John* 8.4f.

21 *Matthew* 6.38–42.

22 *Exodus* 21. 12–14, 23–5; *Leviticus* 24.17; *Numbers* 35.16–34; *Deuteronomy* 19.21; Suras 2.178; 5.45; 16.126; etc.

23 *Leviticus* 19.1–13.

24 Arnold Toynbee, *A Study of History*, London, 1939, vol.iv, pp.261ff.

25 M. Ramsey and L. J. Suenens, *The Future of the Christian Church*, London, 1971, p.78.

CHAPTER II THE RELIGIOUS INSTITUTION AND ITS DECLINE

1 This section is mainly based on: H. A. R. Gibb and Harold Bowen, *Islamic Society and the West*, i/2, London, 1957, and Bernard Lewis, *The Emergence of Modern Turkey*, London, 1961.

2 Charles C. Adams, *Islam and Modernism in Egypt*, London, 1933, pp. 259–67; Kenneth Cragg, *Counsels in Contemporary Islam*, Edinburgh, 1965, pp.69–72.

3 Adams, *Islam and Modernism*, pp.253–9; Pierre Cachia, *Ṭāhā Ḥusayn*, London, 1956, pp.58–65.

4 Lewis, *Emergence*, pp.26f.

5 *Ibid.*, p.108.

6 Niyazi Berkes, *The Development of Secularism in Turkey*, Montreal, 1964, p.187.

7 S. Abul Aʿla Maududi, *The Sick Nations of the Modern Age*, Lahore, 1966, p.15 (lecture delivered in 1935 and published as a pamphlet by Islamic Research Academy, Karachi).

8 Nikki Keddie (ed), *Scholars, Saints and Sufis*, Berkeley, 1972, pp. 204–9.

CHAPTER III THE BEGINNINGS OF ISLAMIC RESURGENCE

1 Malise Ruthven, *Islam in the World*, Harmondsworth, 1984, p. 289.

2 Zahra Freeth and H. V. F. Winstone, *Explorers of Arabia*, London, 1978, pp.237, 284.

3 Laurens van der Post, *Jung and the Story of Our Time*, London, 1978, p.125.

4 Charles C. Adams, *Islam and Modernism in Egypt: A Study of the Modern Reform Movement inaugurated by Muhammad ʿAbduh*, London, 1933. This American scholar is not to be confused with the later Canadian scholar Charles J. Adams.

5 Muḥammad ʿAbduh, *The Theology of Unity (Risālat at-Tawḥid)*, Translated by Ishaq Musaʾad and Kenneth Cragg, London, 1965.

6 *Encyclopaedia of Islam*², articles al-Bannāʾ (J. M. B. Jones), al-Ikhwān al-Muslimūn (G. Delanoue); Ruthven, *Islam in the World*, pp.310–21; Olivier Carré and Gérard Michaud, *Les Frères Musulmans*, Paris, 1983.

7 Mawdudi, *Towards Understanding Islam*, Lahore, 1960 (first published 1940). See also: Kenneth Cragg, *Counsels in Contemporary Islam*, Edinburgh, 1965, pp.120–4; Ruthven, *Islam in the World*, pp.326–34.

8 *Towards Understanding Islam*, p.13.

9 S. Abdul Aʿla Maududi, *The Sick Nations of the Modern Age*, Lahore, 1966, p.13.

10 *Ibid.*, p.10.

11 *Ibid.*, p.11f.

12 *Ibid.*, p.8.

13 Mawdudi, *The Economic Problem of Man and its Islamic Solution*, Lahore, 1966, p.33; this was a lecture delivered in 1941.

14 *Ibid.*, p.35.

15 Muhammad Zafrulla Khan, *Muhammad, Seal of the Prophets*, London, 1980.

16 Muhammad Zafrulla Khan, *Islam, its Meaning for Modern Man*, New York, 1962.

17 *Ibid.* p.90.

18 Use has also been made of the article Aḥmadiyya in *Encyclopaedia of Islam*² and *The Encyclopaedia of Religion* and the obituary of Zafrulla Khan in *The Times*, 4.9.85.

CHAPTER IV THE LIBERAL SEARCH FOR A NEW IDENTITY

1 Wilfred Cantwell Smith, *Modern Islam in India*, Lahore, 1943; revised edition, London, 1946.
2 Delivered in 1945; published Chicago, 1947.
3 Kenneth Cragg, *Counsels in Contemporary Islam*, Edinburgh, 1965.
4 New edition, London, 1922; grew out of *The Life and Teachings of Muhammad*, published in 1890.
5 Fazlur Rahman, *Islam and Modernity*, Chicago, 1982, p. 92–8.
6 *Uluslararasi Birinci Islam Araṣtirmalari Sempozyumu* (report), Izmir, 1985.
7 Alexander S. Cudsi in James P. Piscatori (ed), *Islam in the Political Process*, Cambridge, 1983, p.52.
8 See Ruth McVey in Piscatori (ed.), *Islam in the Political Process*, pp.199–225; also Fazlur Rahman, *Islam and Modernity*, pp. 125–9; B. J. Boland, *The Struggle of Islam in Modern Indonesia*, The Hague, 1971, and various articles.
9 See Arkoun's books: *Pour une critique de la raison islamique; Lectures du Coran*, Paris, 1982; *Essais sur la pensée islamique*, 3rd edn, Paris, 1984.

CHAPTER V THE SELF-IMAGE AND CONTEMPORARY PROBLEMS

1 In *Muslim World*, lxxvii (1987), p.67.
2 Clifford Geertz, 'Religion as a Cultural System', in Robert Bocock and Kenneth Thompson (eds), *Religion and Ideology*, Manchester, 1985, p.67.
3 Gerard W. Hughes, *God of Surprises*, London, 1985, pp.16f.,21.
4 Ziauddin Sardar in *Hamdard Islamicus*, ix (1986), p.30.
5 W. Montgomery Watt, *Islam and Christianity Today*, London, 1983, pp.23f.; 'iconic' is suggested on p.119.
6 *Matthew* 2.1–13. Suras 2.125–9; 3.97; 14.35–7; 22.26–9.
7 Further discussed in *Islam and Christianity Today*, p.98.
8 See W. Montgomery Watt, *The Formative Period of Islamic Thought*, Edinburgh, 1973, p.284.
9 Sura 23.88.
10 E.g. *Islam and Christianity Today*, p.63.
11 For details see W. Montgomery Watt, *Muhammad at Mecca*,

Oxford, 1953, pp. 72–85; *Muhammad Prophet and Statesman*, London, 1961, pp.46–55.

12 See W. Montgomery Watt, 'Belief in a "High God" in pre-Islamic Mecca', *Journal of Semitic Studies*, xvi (1971), pp.35–40; 'The Qur'ān and Belief in a "High God" ', *Der Islam*, vi (1979), pp.205–11.

13 See Watt, *Muhammad at Mecca*, pp. 62–72.

14 *2 Samuel* 11.

15 Suras 3.48; 5.10.

16 W. Montgomery Watt, *Muhammad at Medina*, Oxford, 1956, p. 240.

17 Ibn Hishām, Göttingen, 1858, pp. 341–3; Watt, *Islamic Political Thought*, Edinburgh, 1968, pp. 130–4; Watt, *Muhammad at Medina*, pp. 221–5.

18 Watt, *Islamic Political Thought*, p.14.

19 See M. Arkoun in *Islamochristiana*, xii (1986), p.141.

20 In Mawdudi, *Islam, its Meaning and Message*, ed. Khurshid Ahmad, London, 1976, p.161.

21 Watt, *Islamic Political Thought*, pp.35–40.

22 Kenneth Cragg, *Counsels in Contemporary Islam*, pp. 21–3.

23 M. Arkoun in *Islamochristiana*, xii, p.151.

24 In Mawdudi, *Islam, its Meaning and Message*, p.161.

25 M. Ali Kattani in Kh. Ahmad and Z. I. Ansari (eds), *Islamic Perspectives: Studies in Honour of . . . Mawdūdī*, Leicester/Jeddah, 1979, p.242.

25 Suras 8.74; 9.20; 2.218.

27 Mawdudi, *Towards Understanding Islam*, Lahore, 1960, p.150.

28 *Encyclopaedia of Islam*², article Djihād (E.Tyan).

29 Khomeini, *Light of the Path*, published by Jihad-e-sazandegi (Jihad for Construction), Tehran, 1982, p.54f.

30 V. S. Naipaul, *Among the Believers: an Islamic Journey*, Harmondsworth, 1982, p.88.

31 H. A. R. Gibb, *Modern Trends in Islam*, Chicago, 1947, p.113.

32 *Ibid.*, p.121.

33 James P. Piscatori (ed.), *Islam in the Political Process*, Cambridge, 1983, p.26, quoted from Sami Jawhar, *Al-Mawta yakakallamun*, Cairo, 1977, p.138.

34 Khomeini, *Light of the Path*, pp.90, 106.

35 *Encyclopaedia of Islam*², article Djihād.

36 Fazlur Rahman, *Islam and Modernity, Transformation of an Intellectual Tradition*, Chicago 1982, p.8.
37 Norman Anderson, *Law Reform in the Muslim World*, London, 1976, p.45.
38 Rahman, *Islam and Modernity*, p.142.
39 *Ibid.*, pp.150, 156f.
40 Faruq Sherif, *A Guide to the Contents of the Qur'ān*, London, 1985, p.4.
41 *International Journal of Middle East Studies*, xviii (1986), pp.135–64.
42 S. M. Sayeed in *Hamdard Islamicus*, ix/3 (1986), pp.67,74.
43 *Islamochristiana* ix (1983).
44 English text in *Islamochristiana*, ix, pp.103–20.
45 See Valerie J. Hoffman-Ladd, 'Polemics on the Modesty and Segregation of Women in Contemporary Egypt', in *International Journal of Middle East Studies*, xix (1987), pp.23–50.
46 *Ibid.*, p.34.
47 *Ibid.*, p.28.
48 Naipaul, *Among the Believers*, p.352.
49 See: Jacques Waardenburg, 'World Religions as seen in the Light of Islam', in A. T. Welch and P. Cachia, *Islam: Past Influence and Present Challenge*, Edinburgh, 1979, pp.245–75.
50 Naipaul, *Among the Believers*, p.14.
51 *Imam*, iv/1 (Jan.1984), p.40.
52 See *Die Zeit*, 29.3.85.

CHAPTER VI THE IRANIAN EXPERIENCE

1 S. Husain M. Jafri, *The Origins and Early Development of Shi'a Islam*, London, 1979; the quotation is from p.203; use has also been made throughout the chapter of Nikki Keddie, *Roots of Revolution: an Interpretive History of Modern Iran*, New Haven, 1981.
2 See: W. O. Beeman in Nikki Keddie (ed.), *Religion and Politics in Iran*, New Haven, 1983, p.195.
3 English translation: *Occidentosis, a Plague from the West*, tr. by R. Campbell, Berkeley, 1984.
4 A. Shariati, *Hajj*, tr. by Somayyah and Yaser, Bedford, Ohio, 1977, p.130; also in *Imam*, iv/1, p.46.
5 Keddie (ed.), *Religion and Politics in Iran*, pp.218–20.

6 *Ibid.*, pp.140f.
7 *Ibid.*, p.166; quoted from a collection of his writings, *Islam and Revolution*, tr. H. Algar, Berkeley, 1981, p.28.
8 H. A. R. Gibb, *Modern Trends in Islam*, Chicago, 1947, p.121.
9 Mary Hegland in Keddie (ed.), *Religion and Politics*, p.226.

CHAPTER VII EPILOGUE

1 H. A. R. Gibb, *Modern Trends in Islam*, Chicago, 1947, p.124f.
2 V. S. Naipaul, *Among the Believers: an Islamic Journey*, Harmondsworth, 1982, pp.125–35.

BIBLIOGRAPHY

ʿAbduh, Muḥammad, *The Theology of Unity*, translated by I. Musa'ad and K. Cragg, London, Allen & Unwin, 1965.

Adams, Charles C., *Islam and Modernism in Egypt*, London, Oxford University Press, 1933.

Ahmad, Khurshid (ed.), *Islam, its Meaning and Message*, London, Islamic Council of Europe, 1976.

Ahmad, Kh. and Ansari, Z. I. (eds.), *Islamic Perspectives: Studies in Honour of . . . Mawdūdī*, Leicester, Islamic Foundation, 1979.

Ameer Ali, Syed, *The Spirit of Islam*, London, Christophers, 1922.

Anderson, Norman, *Law Reform in the Muslim World*, London, Athlone Press, 1976.

Arkoun, Mohammed, *Lectures du Coran*, Paris, Maisonneuve, 1982.

Arkoun, Mohammed, *Essais sur la pensée islamique*, 3rd edn, Paris, Maisonneuve, 1984.

Arkoun, Mohammed, *Pour une critique de la raison islamique*, Paris, Maisonneuve, 1984.

Arkoun, Mohammed, 'Émergences et problèmes dans le monde musulman contemporain', *Islamochristiana*, 12 (1986), 135–61.

Barral, J. M. (ed.), *Orientalia Hispanica*, vol. 1, Leiden, Brill, 1974.

Berkes, Niyazi, *The Development of Secularism in Turkey*, Montreal, 1964.

Bocock, R. and Thompson, K. (eds.), *Religion and Ideology*, Manchester, Manchester University Press, 1985.

Boland, B. J., *The Struggle of Islam in Modern Indonesia*, The Hague, Mouton, 1971.

Cachia, Pierre, *Ṭāhā Ḥusayn*, London, Luzac, 1956.

Carré, O. and Michaud, G., *Les frères musulmans*, Paris, Gallimard/Julliard, 1983.

Cragg, Kenneth, *Counsels in Contemporary Islam*, Edinburgh University Press, 1965.

Encyclopaedia of Islam, 2nd edn., English, Leiden, Brill, 1960.

Encyclopaedia of Religion, The, New York, Macmillan, 1987.

Freeth, Z., and Winstone, H. V. F., *Explorers of Arabia*, London, 1978.

Gibb, H. A. R., *Modern Trends in Islam*, Chicago, University of Chicago Press, 1947.

Gibb, H. A. R., and Bowen, H., *Islamic Society and the West*, i/2, London, Oxford University Press, 1957.

Gibbon, Edward, *The History of the Decline and Fall of the Roman Empire*, several editions.

Hamdard Islamicus, quarterly, Karachi, Hamdard Foundation (Pakistan).

Hoffman-Ladd, Valerie J., 'Polemics on the Modesty and Segregation of Women in Contemporary Egypt', *International Journal of Middle East Studies*, xix (1987), 23–50.

Hughes, Gerard W., *God of Surprises*, London, Darton, Longman & Todd, 1985.

Ibn Hishām, *Sīra*, ed. F. Wüstenfeld, Göttingen, Dieterich, 1858–60.

Imam, monthly, London, Iranian Embassy.

Islamochristiana, annual, Rome, Pontificio Istituto di Studi Arabi e d'Islamistica.

Juynboll, G. H. A., *The Authenticity of the Tradition Literature: Discussions in Modern Egypt*, Leiden, Brill, 1969,

Keddie, Nikki (ed.), *Scholars, Saints and Sufis*, Berkeley, University of California Press, 1972.

Keddie, Nikki, *Roots of Revolution: an Interpretive History of Modern Iran*, New Haven, Yale, 1981.

Keddie, Nikki (ed.), *Religion and Politics in Iran*, New Haven, Yale, 1983.

Küng, Hans and others, *Christianity and the World Religions: Paths to Dialogue with Islam, Hinduism and Buddhism*, New York, Doubleday, 1986.

Küng, Hans, 'Christianity and World Religions: the Dialogue with Islam as One Model'; with Responses by Seyyed Hossein Nasr and others, *Muslim World*, 77 (1987), 80–136.

Kuran, Timur, 'The Economic System in Contemporary Islamic Thought: Interpretation and Assessment', *International Journal of Middle East Studies*, xviii (1986), 135–64.

Lewis, Bernard, *The Emergence of Modern Turkey*, London, Oxford University Press, 1961.

Lewis, Bernard, *The Muslim Discovery of Europe*, London, Weidenfeld & Nicolson, 1982.

Massignon, Louis, *Opera Minora*, vol.1, Beirut, Dar al-Maaref, 1963.

Maududi, Abul Aʿla, *Towards Understanding Islam*, 6th edn, Karachi, Islamic Publications, 1960.

Maududi, Abul Aʿla, *The Economic Problem of Man and its Islamic Solution*, 2nd edn, Karachi, Islamic Publications, 1966.

Maududi, Abul Aʿla, *The Sick Nations of the Modern Age*, Karachi, Islamic Publications, 1966.

Naipaul, V. S., *Among the Believers: an Islamic Journey*, Harmondsworth, Penguin Books, 1982.

Nöldeke, Theodor and Schwally, F., *Geschichte des Qorāns*, 2nd edn reprinted, Hildesheim, Olms, 1961.

Piscatori, James P. (ed.), *Islam in the Political Process*, Cambridge, Cambridge University Press, 1983.

Rahman, Fazlur, *Islam and Modernity: Transformation of an Intellectual Tradition*, Chicago, University of Chicago Press, 1982.
Ramsey, M. and Suenens, L. J., *The Future of the Christian Church*, London, 1971.
Risalat al-Jihad, monthly, Tripoli (Libya), Islamic Call Society.
Ruthven, Malise, *Islam in the World*, Harmondsworth, Penguin Books, 1984.
Shariati, Ali, *Hajj*, translated by Somayyah and Yaser, Bedford (Ohio), Free Islamic Literatures, 1977.
Sherif, Faruq, *A Guide to the Contents of the Qur'an*, London, Ithaca Press, 1985.
Toynbee, A. J., *A Study of History*, vol. iv, London, Oxford University Press, 1939.
Uluslararasi Birinci Islam Arastirmalari Sempozyumu, Izmir, Dokuz Eylül Üniversitesi, 1985.
van der Post, Laurens, *Jung and the Story of our Time*, Harmondsworth, Penguin Books, 1978.
Waardenburg, Jacques, 'World Religions as seen in the Light of Islam', in A. T. Welch and P. Cachia, *Islam: Past Influence and Present Challenge*, Edinburgh, Edinburgh University Press, 1979.
Watt, W. M., *Muhammad at Mecca*, Oxford, Clarendon Press, 1953.
Watt, W. M., *Muhammad at Medina*, Oxford, Clarendon Press 1956.
Watt, W. M., 'Created in His Image', *Transactions of the Glasgow University Oriental Society*, xviii (1959–60), 38–49.
Watt, W. M., *Muhammad Prophet and Statesman*, London, Oxford Univeristy Press, 1961.
Watt, W. M., *Islamic Political Thought*, Edinburgh, Edinburgh University Press, 1968.
Watt, W. M., 'Belief in a "High God" in pre-Islamic Mecca', *Journal of Semitic Studies*, xvi (1971), 35–40.
Watt, W. M., *The Formative Period of Islamic Thought*, Edinburgh, Edinburgh University Press, 1973.
Watt, W. M., 'The Qur'ān and Belief in a "High God" ', *Der Islam*, 56 (1979), 205–11.
Watt, W. M., *Islam and Christianity Today*, London, Routledge & Kegan Paul, 1984.
Watt, W. M., *Muhammad's Mecca: History from the Qur'ān*, Edinburgh, Edinburgh University Press, 1988.
Zafrulla Khan, M., *Islam, its Meaning for Modern Man*, New York, Harper & Row, 1962.
Zafrulla Khan, M., *Muhammad, Seal of the Prophets*, London, Routledge & Kegan Paul, 1980.

INDEX